BUNDERCHOOK STARWORD POET 'REVIVAL'

Ram-rod Edition

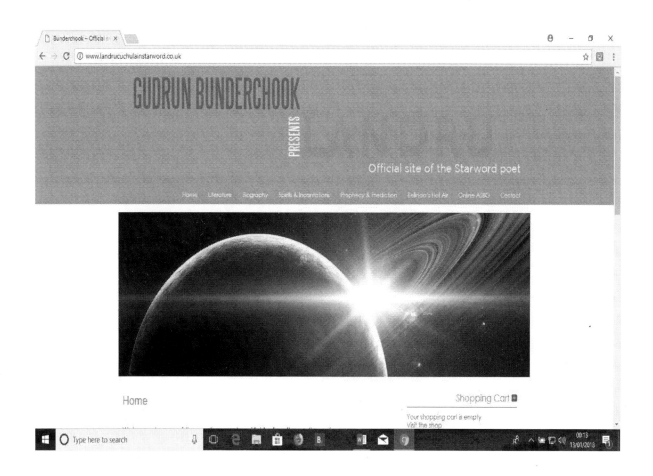

Intro

By popular demand SOP has returned with a new collection of short stories, acts of sedition and utter lawlessness. If we get through this century without a major world war I will be greatly surprised. Do not be too shocked by anything you read. You can always yell out if you start to feel under the weather.

Copyright A G Enterprises 2018   Paris edition

WITH EXTRACTS FROM THE WORLD-FAMOUS WEB-SITE:

www.landrucuchulain.starword.co.uk

N B Required reading for all minor Quaker Poets.

CONTENTS

GERARD NERVAL'S CANDLE

John's brother Ken,
Drunk on the street again,
Leapt from a bridge, into the path,
Of an on-coming freight.

Peter, my friend, who lent me his bike,
To free-wheel down the hill to the chippy,
One summer.

Members of an exclusive band,
Whose fee was everything they had.

The Stranger who came on the news,
Discovered in a hotel room,
Hanging from a balloon,
And the girl from the gym,
Who always seemed so happy...

I carried my jewels,
Swinging in red and ochre,
Over the back of a donkey,
To the grave of my father,
Who seemed just as keen to go,
Without ever saying goodbye.

The Swarm's hierarchy of industrious establishment turpats, who are the *actual foul* Scythians in all of this, looting like leeches on the active artery, the parasite "equality", a strangulating hernia raping the function of emote, whose whore surgeons of the retrospect distil sentences mathetically from one to another, as their contrivance interferes with an absolute necessity. *Will provoke them i's passion.* D:Mru am old world prophet once had that, "he who is without guilt let him cast the first stone." Or as the North American Indians used to accuse "do not judge a man until you have walked to him in his moccasins" and since we'd fear crosses the same river twice.

Yet at the moment of impact we'd agents de provocateurs, painting with the brushstrokes of our words, are under attack from telluric hellcats and crusading Amazons, who would castrate us in a jar of muriatic acid, if fortune favoured them. If we're indeed *to judge a goat by its coat,* then I can only urge the *outlaws* to turn the board and wreck the table.

If the Clansmen laud to the skies are a thorn in your side, then be as a dart in their tribunal, gut, become what you are, burst the chains of your imprisonment, and play the starring role, as a *battering ram,* to wooden laws and castle gates. Realize your fondest fain to fertilize *our horrida bella* between the sky and the earth, and reassort hyperion influence in the universe, overthrow the widespread perfury of the masses who would steal our assimilate thunder and rob us of the golden dawn to come, learn *how to correctly insult* a *Milesian woman.*

However, if you are of the people, run for the larder, little soldier, I am about to switch on the light.

landru Dublin March 1989

FOREWARNED

quem tu, qua lubet, ut libet, mane to
quantum his, hi, si sit foris para'am.

Catullus c.50 B.C.

How is directly, *the wired Milesian woman.*

This book is a statement on the demise of innocence, and a swipe at the bog strutters two-faced palter of lies, where vengeful Eros degenerated into vice.

The truth should forgive the expression 'al, change out' as an enchiridion of contemporary Scylla and internecine conflict, where 'to censor nothing is an act of love'.

This deviant desire, which turns us bastard beauty, invokes the *Judas kiss of morality* above the jesuitry of human rights, inherited from discredited ideals, to energize the pioneer spirit in our flying man to higher and greater deeds of disorder, to boldly odyssey where no bird has flown before, emplaned by the Isidra's lust for punishment, whose inner chord recalls its wayward beast, and then feasts on the carrion. For even fickle Ge must teem that warp within the human mollusc will lead to strife outside the home. But this sucked orange can't which shanghai's an increasingly powerful sex drive cannot invoke at any particular whim in time, by the 'divine right of government', through its mutant benchmen of *Dante* President proclaiming as a pit of abiding folly, he'd child like error of crime will, the double headed Cyclops of crime and punishment.

Home

Welcome to one of the most unusual and intriguing sites on the net.

The Literature section comprises a number of different *HIVES* each containing a selection of short stories, poems, and political satire.
There is also a section -
involving **Prophecy** and **Prediction**, **Spells** and **Invocations**.
You can also order your own personalised **ASBO**.
I have long considered writing to be a *form of art*. The Artwork section contains pages from the *infamous* 'THUNDERBUCK RAM.'

BELINDA'S HOT AIR gives participants of the site the opportunity to express their views on a very diverse range of subjects. By clicking on the heading, you can add your own comments, but you need to be signed in to **Facebook**. '

A place to pour your scorn upon the world.'

FIRST CONTACT is a forum for new untested artforms and experimental writing.

In an age of increasing state control and monitoring your general comments and feedback are positively encouraged.
Our freedom of speech and liberal values have to be permanently fought for or else they are lost.

Live dangerously and to your heart be true!

Proxima Centauri Alpha
L0+4A

EXTRACTS FROM THE SITE ARE NOW AVAILABLE AT AMAZON UK: BUNDERCHOOK STARWORD POET. New titles and editions: Widening Underground, Criminal Tendencies, Offensive Behaviour, Alien Intelligence, Odd bent Coppers, Natural Surveillance, Trades of the Toadman, **Dance of the red-crowned Prince, King Simon's yellow bull-frog, Thunderbuck Ram I -IV.** *Curse of the Wallingford Stalker.*

LATEST DROSS ON THE WILL

Pain-in-the-butt.

Heard mum kicking off again tonight. I have not said anything to *Nurse Nosey-britches*. She was talking to Aunty Jenny and Uncle Kevin on Skype. Mum told them that you wanted to buy me a house from the money left in her will. This is extremely good news as long as you mean it. There would be nothing to stop you going back on your word of course.

Mum: "it's my will, not Genevieve's. I want what I want in it. It's my will not hers!"
"Genevieve rang off and was really nasty to me on the phone today."

Aunty Jenny: "are you sure you are all alone Margaret? You want to keep these papers safe so no one else can see them. Buy yourself a little safe to keep them in!"
"Don't let Genevieve get Power of Attorney whatever you do. She could turn you out of your own home! Get your will done properly so that you get to say where you want the money to go, not where Genevieve wants it to go."
"You can leave your money to the Dog's Home if you want to."
"You need to do it now. That way you won't even have to talk to either Genevieve or Andrew about it. There won't be any fighting about what's in it. We worry about you. Get it sorted out soon. Do it for us Margaret."

Mum said that she didn't have anyone she could talk to, unlike Jenny and Kevin...
"I've had to ask Diane to take me into hospital. I have a car but I can't use it."
Mum got a little exasperated:
"My health has to come first. The Doctor says I have all sorts of horrid things in my throat."
Mum said that things were always walking out of drawers. I presume that's another reference to me being light-fingered.
"Why did I have two such rotten children? After all I've done for them."

Aunty Jenny agreed with mum that everything should be split fairly down the middle, which of course is the decent thing to do.

Mum said that she had "always been good with money," and that she had three pensions. The one from Bradford Council she didn't even use.

Mum told them she had once worked as a Detective before she was a teacher and used to love going around arresting people.

She told them that I was always stealing things from the house. She also said that her college scarf had disappeared from the room where you had slept not that long ago.

Mum said she had sent Heather a lot of money towards a house.

*I have found mum's hospital appointment book on a chair in 'your' room. That is one of the things I am supposed to have stolen.

Uncle Kevin: "Margaret, how would you like to come over to Canada if Jenny came for you and brought you with her?"

"Are you sure Heather has go the cheque (for £10,000). Have you rung her to make sure it has arrived alright?"

*I can't understand why mum has to send Heather a deposit for a house when both her and Dara have good well paid professional jobs. The arguments we have had over using the dish-washer!

NB Incidentally, I over-heard all the conversation you had with the Copper that time as well.

November 27 2017

Dear Aunty Jenny and Uncle Kevin,

My mum has asked me to write and say thank you for my hat, which I have worn, and which keeps me warm in the winter. Thank you for bringing it for me. You have obviously noticed my lack of a good enough thatch.

I hope you don't mind me mentioning a few other things while I'm about it. Could I reassure you that I have not been taking anything from my mum. She has been accusing me of this for years. For months she accused me of taking her bread-knife each time I visited, so I bought her a new one, only to find the old one still in the garage.

I don't think it's any secret that mum gave away Keith's expensive hi-fi equipment away to a man who 'd just called at the door. Mum seems alright on the phone or in company, but that's the way it really is. It feels as if people are picking on me when they don't believe me.

Today she accused me of taking some gold medallions from a drawer. I don't have any idea what she is talking about or where on earth they are.

The truth is, a lot of things do keep disappearing, and from my room! I had to replace a camera she had taken last year, and she still hasn't given me back the glasses she took from my bag last week.

We were doing some car-boot sales this summer with her full agreement. At the last one the car broke down so I had to call a garage. The mechanic said there was a problem with the battery and alternator caused by 'wear-and-tear,' and that they both needed replacing at the same time. Since then mum has hidden the car at a neighbour's house (but brought it back again for Gen to use when she came over). She held me responsible for the battery and alternator even though I told her what the garage had said.

I have spoken to my sister about the will. She told me that when mum leaves everything to her in the will she will "buy me a house to live in."

She once told me that she thought all the Watson women were 'mad.' I may be getting old, but I still aren't a fool. My sister is a professional 'Historian.' She's good at 're-writing' history anyway.

I honestly don't want any hand-outs. I really don't want anything from anyone, but life is going to be even tougher without anywhere to live.

I did overhear Gen arguing on the phone with my mum again the other day. My mum kept saying that it was her will to write what she wanted in it. She also told my sister that she did not want her to have 'Power of Attorney.' She said that was "completely out of the question."

My sister can be very insistent and is used to getting her own way. I know that you and Kevin communicate with her regularly, especially Uncle Kevin. I also know that Gen and Uncle Chris having been putting pressure on my mum to get rid of me as soon as she can, but unlike my sister or Uncle Chris, I don't have anywhere else to live and would be out on the street.

I continue to offer my mum support whenever she needs it. As you probably know, I worked as a live-in Carer for some of my life, so I am well used to all the problems this entails.

It is very hard to get through to my mum sometimes. Genevieve thinks this is due to 'her illness.' The only way you will really get her to do anything is to be there with her yourself. I wish you good luck in your endeavours.

I totally agree that it would be both unjust and unfair for my mother to treat us differently. I grew up alongside my sister, and although I was very badly treated by my so-called father, I never felt as if she was any better than me. As you rightly imply, getting the will done (without Genevieve influencing the proceedings) and finally wording it as my mum wanted, is a pressing priority. I don't really want to interfere. My mum went into Norwich with my sister the last time it was done and I was not even spoken to.

It was a kind offer to take my mum over to Canada for a while but please don't let her fall out of the aircraft and into the Atlantic on the way. It just goes to show Aunty Jenny, that you are both Christians at heart even though you don't always show it. I'm sure she would appreciate a holiday. As your own mother knew, it can be very tiring ordering everyone about and playing tricks. Playing one off against another is a family trait?

Usually when my mum goes away for a break it gives me the chance to clean up all the house and do any spare jobs that need doing. I do one room at a time and make sure it is completely spick-and-span for when she returns. I used to go and pick her up when she came back from her trips but that is not an option at the moment.

I hope that after reading my words you are wiser and more understanding of the situation here. I know we are both sensitive people underneath who really want to get on and make some progress without animosity or the holding of grudges for things long since passed.

On Thursday I have to go in to see a Consultant about an operation on my knees. Have been quite poorly over the last few years.

Do you remember 7, Clara Street?

Sincerely,
All the best,
BLUNDERCHOOK BLACKSHEEP

THEIR REPLY:

'We have read your note *this time,* but we don't think it's appropriate to discuss Margaret with the likes of you. We just care about her.'

'When are you going to leave?'

Never!

Dear Celebrity Jungle (Ant and Dec),

I am a **Writer** and **Artist** living and working in Norfolk.

During the last three years myself and my partner have never missed a single episode of 'In the Jungle,' and have grown to really like that *pair of Jokers*.

I wonder if you mind me sending in a few ideas about some more games you could use for the programme to make it even more outstanding.

This is just a few ideas I've had today.

A <u>Camp Stranger/Ranger</u>

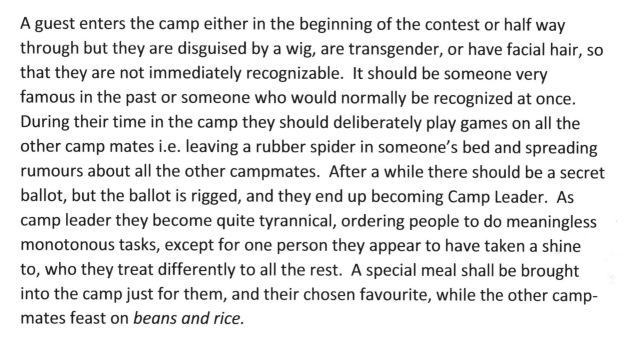

A guest enters the camp either in the beginning of the contest or half way through but they are disguised by a wig, are transgender, or have facial hair, so that they are not immediately recognizable. It should be someone very famous in the past or someone who would normally be recognized at once. During their time in the camp they should deliberately play games on all the other camp mates i.e. leaving a rubber spider in someone's bed and spreading rumours about all the other campmates. After a while there should be a secret ballot, but the ballot is rigged, and they end up becoming Camp Leader. As camp leader they become quite tyrannical, ordering people to do meaningless monotonous tasks, except for one person they appear to have taken a shine to, who they treat differently to all the rest. A special meal shall be brought into the camp just for them, and their chosen favourite, while the other camp-mates feast on *beans and rice.*

A famous Writer, Artist, or Musician would be a good choice. Someone with a mischievous sense of humour, yet who could appear serious.

When they first arrive in camp they should be given menial and degrading tasks until they find the *gold nugget* hidden on the jungle floor.

B FALSE <u>IDENTITY</u>

The *'lookalike'* of a very famous person should arrive in camp, either at the beginning or part way through. The lookalike acts very like the famous celebrity in every way they can, including talking about some of the things they are famous for. They should receive a phone call while they are in the jungle from (a fake) i.e. President Trump (for instance) "Mr President!" who asks how they are coping, tells them he is watching the show, and makes comments on certain other contestants.

The lookalike spreads rumours round camp about someone being in there who are not who they say.

Part way through the camp the real person is swapped with the lookalike, and they continue to remain in camp as normal, and act as if they have been there all the time.

C HURDLES

Using a pole made into a horse the contestants have to ride over various obstacles and fences, with water hazards to win the race for their team.

D GENERAL KNOWLEDGE

Contestants have to answer general knowledge questions about their fellow camp-mates with rewards to the highest scorers. Each contestant has to share a secret (which has to be true) with their fellow camp mates. It has to be something embarrassing which they have never told anyone else before. At the end of the game they have to say whether the story is really true. If they have been lying or have made it up their food rations are taken away.

E ODD ONE OUT

One of the camp-mates deliberately loses their task and can be seen stealing food from the others. They also acquire a reputation for leaving the toilet and shower in a dirty state. The idea is to get all the other camp-mates picking on this one person to see just how much compassion and forgiveness they have.

F THREE TEAMS (Tarzans, Kings, and Ape-men)

Three teams compete to throw coloured sponges at two cardboard cut-outs of ANT AND DEC. The scores are added up at the end and the winners get to eat rice and beans for the rest of the week.

Game time: ten minutes.

Or the time it takes for you to count all your two fingers.

G HOSPITAL

Some of the camp-mates return from a foray into the jungle only to find one of their camp-mates being taken away on a stretcher, with the sound of a helicopter overhead. It should really be the person who has become the most disliked. A lot of fuss should be made about what has happened to them as they are taken away. In the morning they should arise from their bed as normal as if nothing has happened and act as if they are as fit as a fiddle.

Get Ant blind drunk and leave him in charge of a motor vehicle.

Abbot and Costello

Had a visit from Abbot and Costello, another pair of goons, last month.
They wanted to inspect my computer and look in my bedroom.
They asked me what I was doing for Christmas and why I had been so silly filming other members of their tribe when they came round to poke fun at me.
"Why do you think it all started?" asked Costello.
Mum went to make them a cup of tea and get some cream buns.
"Because I was unhappy," I said. I have fallen into the trap of answering their stupid questions before. It was the best summary I could think of to shut their silly traps.

OVER FIFTIES DATING

Hello!

Thank you for taking the time to look at *my profile*...(can you spot any mistakes?) my profile is probably v different to others so I hope you enjoy my sense of humour and assertiveness to avoid wasting each other's time so please ensure you have read all of it prior to messaging me in case I may have changed it which is highly likely with the more I learn about online dating and common decency or lack of in some cases...no subterfuge please

Still reading? Great!   I like seeing profiles with...

Decent recent photos of you...no tongues poking out, no fish, no alcohol, no sunglasses, no bikes etc just you and... Your real age   No Smokers   No 'pretending' to be the owner of a convertible sports car or mansion

Not playing with balls, which appear to get smaller with age...for example footballs, snooker and or golf etc

I am more of a boaty type person...still reading? Fantastic!

I am not really attracted to men who wear sports team strips, particularly whilst they slouch in a sunken sofa seat on a Saturday afternoon eating a kebab dripping its grease onto an exposed impregnated looking stomach whilst their dog is permitted to lick it off in the process of shouting at footy on telly with a tinny of alcohol followed by eproctophilia for dessert   Collecting drift wood on a Saturday afternoon is far more enjoyable to me

Still reading? Wonderful!

I will now continue by adding what I am interested in...humour to start with...

I like a talll, distinctive, kind, caring, interesting, artistic, creative man who is available to spend quality time with me, especially on a weekend to appreciate nature and the elements whether it's from in or outside or IN!

Do you like a woman who is tall, slim, with long blond/greying hair who prefers a more natural appearance (as I believe make up is for highlighting ones features rather then covering attractiveness) Still reading? Fabulous!

I enjoy dressing *appropriately* although I'm more inclined to be creatively productive with my hands rather than investing into too much glamour such as nail polish... I'm not the type of person to do so on a regular basis...feeling comfortable is more important than anything Still reading? Superb!

Do you like unusual things? I like eclectic... Hand made Inventions dildos Eco lifestyle Wood burners Solar energy   Log cabins   Boats – long, narrow, yachts, any! Starry nights Aurora Borealis Board games

The Green Dragon

I respect our planet and I prefer anything organic and cruelty free so I tend to avoid toxic products if or when I can and prefer bamboo, wood etc rather than plastic, unless it's been recycled

Still reading? Incredible!

As you have kept reading, I hope you decide to message me, if so, please have something interesting to share such as travel, creative or artistic, woodwork etc or... surprise me! Not with unwanted explicit pics and do not ask for any as you will be ignored

Still reading? That's brilliant!

If you are then I look forward to reading your profile and message(s) too as we could be on the same frequency

If not, best of luck and I hope you enjoy dating and find whatever and whoever you're looking for.

Best wishes in 2018 Love, **Muriel x.**

THE WIZARD OF PENDLE

A few years ago, I was invited to work on a farm on the slopes of Pendle Hill, in Lancashire. It belonged to a farmer called 'Eddie Ayres.' He was the strongest man alive at that time and could haul a large tractor out of the mud with just a rope while we teenagers mucked around in the straw. I had been attracted by stories that his farmhouse was actually haunted. We didn't see anything, but we heard plenty, including some footsteps coming down the old rickety steps at night, while we crashed out legless on the downstairs slabs.

On the third night we tramped down the hill to Barley where a small pub awaited our custom. A night of drunken revelry followed. We were a strange bunch of lads. I never really felt like one of the gang. My new silver cigarette lighter was stolen but I couldn't find out who had taken it.

As the pub filled to almost bursting I offered to demonstrate my skills as a Magician. With just a beer glass and a box of matches I said I could lift up a whole wooden table without even touching it.

My audience simply laughed. 'It was impossible!' they cried. Each of them wagered a nice round tenner that I couldn't do what I claimed.

I assembled my tools: taking a deep drink I downed almost all my pint, leaving just a small amount of beer in the bottom. I tossed this over a beer mat on the table and made sure it was nicely soaked in. Then I placed a shilling on top of the beer-mat. I opened my box of matches to England's glory, and began breaking off their red heads: nine in all, and lay them on top of the shilling. I finished my pint and placed it up-turned on top of the beer-mat, covering the shilling and match heads. Next, I lifted the lid of the pint glass at one corner and quickly set fire to the matches in the centre, throwing the pint glass quickly back, and pressing its lip into the beer mat. A plume of flame and smoke appeared inside the glass. Someone from the bar staff went to fetch the landlord.

I grabbed hold of the beer glass near the top with both hands and lifted the table clear off the ground. It was just then that the landlord appeared. He looked extremely worried and stared down at the table. I invited him to replicate my act. That's the last I saw of him before we vacated the premises.

We vanished back to Yorkshire with a posse of police-cars trying to locate our whereabouts on the misty rain drenched moors.

When we returned to the village a few months after we were not allowed back in the Malt Shovel. I heard that they had to smash the glass to get it off the table and that shortly after the Landlord's wife had run off with a man from the brewery.

Why is this happening to you? xx

21 NOVEMBER 02:45

I don't know
But I'm sick drew
I don't even tell my friends
Yeah and some more than others I noticed
I haven't been on I'm really sick since Thursday

I was at my doc and waited outside w a new abscess u know that. And I was nauseous and I got worse and felt sicker and I waited I came in and burst out crying and he hugged me and sat me and comforted me and took blood and I was gonna wait while I got just extremely sick and ran to throw up and at the way back outside his door I got worse and his door was open and I went over and climbed to the door cill and said omg I'm so sick ! Help me Christian!! And he flew over and almost carried me to the chair and gave me a diazapham cause my heart was pounding and I don't remember a lot. We made love for hours on his floor. When I got home I went to bed and fell asleep sitting in not even sure I fell asleep. I sat up when I woke again cold as ice over six h later!! And I still get it so I just fall asleep when I write or talk or read. I'm just sick drew and honestly screw-scared. Was due to start filming with Bob...

For u. A few natural pics I didn't put public well not all 😊 hope u like

Hon. I'd marry you if u were buy far not the only boy!! 😳

Don't sell yourself short. Oh yeah women w no brain or nerd 🤓 gene will hate it!! But we love the same things!! I saw on tv a program where they show Tintagel! And also, things from it I tried to film it w no success sadly I thought how you'd love it!! I have a new contract to star in Between the sheets!

Yes we'd be happy I have no doubt and I love the English country in my English country house dresses w loose corsages in white linen. Yes I dress like that. I truly am that natural!

I took 100 100 mg phenobarbital

Then I hid the glass and put one that said 10 mg 20 pieces

I really wanted to die but it would break Bob's heart   he will not leave his wife

Mette Fuglsang von Ribbentrop *to* **Drew Gallagher**

22 November at 18:51 ·

For my bestie, a total sweetheart who puts up w me when I lash out when I'm down. I wonder how many knows how amazing you really are ....? 💜🐾🔔. thank you for being my friend and for being patient w me. Mille agrees! 🐱.

Us

Bc we are interested in the same and are both a bit... well we stand w one foot in the other world and sadly ppl rarely do that. No man can come close to you!

I hope u know what I mean?

I'm really sick so if something were to happen... u should know I do think of you more and more fondly and if I was arranged to be married to you I wouldn't say no.

U are such a total sweetheart xxx

For u

When it's styled it's hot!! But I dare show u me naked u know
And honestly? I still look like that good naked but my stomach is actually a bit smaller
It's odd cause ppl don't know I am really honest in my poems

Also the public ones
I mean I hide behind the words
I can lay naked
U know? Oh, fuk you!

Drew
but love to me is like a pallet stuffed with pins, that drains away my blood for whores to drink...no wonder Baudelaire was banned by the Establishment!

I'm not medically trained in all aspects of health-care, but I think I know what's going on here. You have my sincere condolences!

(Conversations on Face-book shortly before deleting me from her friends list)

HAPPY CHRISTMAS EVERYONE!

According to the bible Methuselah lived to be nine hundred and sixty-nine years old. You would think that a generous and loving God would at least let him make it to a nice round thousand. If only that nasty flood hadn't got in the way!

Bunderchook Starword POET I make it a habit to accept all the bullshit society tells me, don't you?
Like Show More Reactions
· Reply · Just now

Comments

Fire and fury

By <u>ADUMLA</u> | *Published: JANUARY 5, 2018* | *Edit*

Wolfe doesn't have an ounce of credibility in his body. He wasn't even allowed inside the White House, so all his information must have arrived second hand, and we know what that means! Sounds like another Democrat in the pay of the Clinton gang.

Comments

Warboys rapist

By <u>ADUMLA</u> | *Published: JANUARY 5, 2018* | *Edit*

Another thousand rapes which he was never charged with
Served his time but we love labels

Showed remorse but we don't give a fuk
The law can be changed whenever we like it
Bring back *indeterminate sentences* for anyone we don't like the look of
We always tell the truth just like our wonderful Politicians
You'll not get out until we say so
Black cabs best for picking up tramps

Greatest British Monarch

By ADUMLA | *Published: JANUARY 5, 2018* | *Edit*

Henry the eighth is considered by many to be our strongest and most influential king ever. He was a larger than life character who could feast his way through a whole banqueting hall and still have time to shaft his missus. He was a staunch Defender of the Faith, who never missed mass or the opportunity to help himself to one of the Ladies-in-Waiting.

- ✓ A *Prince of the Renaissance* with a good enough up-bringing
- ✓ popular with beggars, gold-diggers and Tykes
- ✓ expert in the annihilation of jousters with a better claim to the throne
- ✓ emptied the monasteries of all their wealth
- ✓ A Christian king with no interest in power whatsoever
- ✓ Aided by an army of spies, snoops and cut-throats
- ✓ could change the law according to his whim
- ✓ closer to God than the average Pope
- ✓ believed the law should serve only him
- ✓ crushed anyone who stood in his way
- ✓ had a thicker neck than most Sumo wrestlers

Point proven then!

Damian Green filthy pervert

By RUMPLESTILTSKIN | Published: DECEMBER 15, 2017 | Edit

It's not long since a retired 'pig,' (that's slang for an interfering do-gooding policeman) snitched to a major newspaper that the First Secretary had viewed 'hard-core' porn on his computer many years ago. A computer which could have been accessed by many people, including the pigs themselves.

At a time of extreme pressure for the Government is this yet another attack from the Anti-Brexiteers. Who is behind this? I doubt if we will ever get to the bottom of it.

To have some porn on your computer is hardly against the law. Some police-officers spend their entire lives tossing away at such material.

One is left to speculate that Mr Green would rather masturbate over a few teenage girls than be involved in doing his job. It must get a bit boring sometimes. I can't blame him at all.

For those of us with even longer memories: Mr Green was threatened with five years in prison by the police when he tried to smuggle out information about certain greedy ass-hole MP's in the great expenses fiasco during November 2008. An army of Pigs whipped round to his house to snoop through all his private possessions and turn his home upside-down on the pretext he had stolen some incriminating documents from the House of Commons. Who needs a 'search warrant,' when you know you are always in the right. Even old love letters between him and his wife were taken away for closer examination.

You ought to watch out Mr Green!

The Pigs really have it in for you mate!

Man with phone put in prison

By <u>USULI TWELVES</u> | *Published: DECEMBER 27, 2017* | <u>*Edit*</u>

An in-mate who tried to phone his pregnant girlfriend on an illegal mobile was placed in custody two days ago after Screws were tipped off by fellow lags. He claimed that the reason he did not use the internal prison phone was because everything he said of any value would be sold to the media by his 'Carers. 'I can't help but feel he was probably telling the truth.

Mucky little fuckers!

My next door neighbours

By <u>PETER SMITH</u> | *Published: JANUARY 8, 2018* | <u>*Edit*</u>

I called next door to ask Janet if she had a new bin time sheet from the council. Her daughter answered. She looked a bit touchy. I'm sure her daughter is a rug-munching Cop; she's so charming and nice on the surface but a complete git underneath.

Reeling her slowly in

By <u>PETER SMITH</u> | *Published: JANUARY 8, 2018* | <u>*Edit*</u>

Brian and Fatso are too lazy to go and visit his mother. His mother swore never to go over there again. They are gradually luring her a bit closer each time they call. It's only a matter of time until Dorcus breaks her word so she can hold the toy again.

Men stronger than women

By PETER SMITH | *Published: JANUARY 8, 2018* | *Edit*

More men survive heart attacks than women. We cannot allow this to continue! There must be complete equality right across the board or we are living in an unjust society.

Entrapment

By BIRD DUNG | *Published: DECEMBER 22, 2017* | *Edit*

For years I thought that police 'entrapment' was against the law. Now you see the pigs doing it all the time. What's changed?

Corrie's Gary Wind-ass told to change his underwear

By USULI TWELVES | Published: DECEMBER 27, 2017 | Edit

News has reached me on the grape-vine that a famous soap star is far too windy for his own good.

Many cast members have complained they were nearly blown off their feet.

I interfered with Ivanka's Bush

By USULI TWELVES | Published: DECEMBER 27, 2017 | Edit

I sent in information which was biased and ill informed

I communicated with a foreign power

I promulgated false news across the world

I tried to influence how citizens would vote

I gave the Republicans a much-needed boost

*But did not help the Clinton gang!

Police cover-up only the tip of the ice-berg

By BIRD DUNG | Published: DECEMBER 20, 2017 | Edit

For years the police have been hiding information useful to the Prosecution because they want to bang-up as many people as they can. Their excuse: 'too much digital information for us to cope with!'
If the Defence do not hand over all the information they have before a trial it is:

1 inadmissible

2 against the law

Who is going to prosecute the Piglets?
Are they going to make their own pork scratchings and put them into bags?
As we have already learnt, any offence involving even the smallest sexual impropriety, is perceived as far more wicked and dangerous than any other crime. This gives the Authorities even more power at their disposal.
I have seen many an Officer cheer when a young man's life has been ruined by ending up in custody, especially if that young man came from a better background, had more than two brain cells to rub together, or was of a different ethnic group.
I suppose an 'apology' is out of the question?
* I know you're watching me by the way!

CONTROLLING BEHAVIOUR CONSIDERED A CRIME

By ADUMLA | Published: DECEMBER 15, 2017 | Edit

Along with bullying, controlling behaviour, especially in a close relationship, will be punishable by law. This will be especially true when you are a designated male with a large pair of testicles hanging between your legs.
Coercive behaviour, when it is reported, will also involve the Authorities paying you a visit (Their kind of controlling and coercive behaviour is fine, because it comes from the law-makers).
"Get up from that stool woman!"
"Do as you are told!"
"Fetch me the whip Alice!"
That's another petty nonsense sneaked onto the Statute book without us knowing. All human behaviour involves a degree of control.
Why isn't anyone standing up to these controlling clowns, or is that against the bullshit too?
* "Please keep this to yourself and don't let anyone know I told you!"

 Bottom of the Form

Why you are being monitored on Facebook

By GODFREY WINKLEBACKER | *Published: DECEMBER 19, 2017* | *Edit*

We are all being monitored on Face-book with the full approval of the Authorities and the Government. Some of us are being monitored every day. Some of us even have our own special 'MONITOR.' Similar to the one we used to have in school, but not as visible, and less accountable. The reason we are being monitored is simple: Big Brother sees us all as a threat, especially anyone with the intelligence to question their behaviour and the zeal to know what they are up to.

"Your algorhythms are grooming the public!"

"You may have radical thoughts which we don't approve of!"

"We don't like your language. We find your words offensive."

"Let's get on with the real business of covering up compensation claims."

"You aren't allowed to use the word 'hate' anymore!"

"I hate you. I do not intend to kill you though."

"It may attract warped individuals with an aggressive world view."

Twitter *are also being blackmailed to do as they are told.*

"Contaminated blood was found in the pig-wagon."

"You are actively promoting racist behaviour."

"You are not doing enough to de-radicalize the general public!"

"You are still not allowed to kill a Tory."

"I'm a Socialist MP, and I know it all!"

"We will *improve* society no matter what you say…"

WHY NOT IDENTIFY YOURSELVES AND STOP HIDING BEHIND THE ASS-HOLE OF THE STATE, YOU INSIDIOUS BASTARDS!

 PORKERS

Affordable housing

By GODFREY WINKLEBACKER | Published: JANUARY 31, 2018 | Edit

Our Green belt land is gradually being swallowed up by an ever-increasing population. The excuse for this is that it provides essential housing for homeless people, and for foreign migrants. How the hell is anyone like that going to afford homes that are hundreds of thousands each and land which is worth one million pounds an acre? Governments could of course, provide them free if they wanted. Governments can do anything they like with the law on their side. Anything except listen!

GOVERNMENT CONSENT FORM

By ADUMLA | Published: DECEMBER 5, 2017 | Edit

All areas must be completed before any sexual activity can begin:

1 Age and social standing.

2 Size and sexual orientation.

3 Ginger, whiskered or shaven.

4 Expected time period/started periods.

5 Turn-ons, clothing or dykes.

6 Performance level.

7 Occupation and knicker elastic.

8 Previous history.

9 Level of expertise.

NB Anyone indulging in fore-play without completing their form will be pilloried and taken the see the Headmistress for a good dressing down.

Comments

**red**

God bless Dennis Wise

By HERPES ZOSTER | Published: DECEMBER 9, 2017 | Edit

I heard on the news today that Dennis Wise has been labelled a 'bully.'
Just after he had shown himself to be a totally different person to the
one that is always being painted. He was intelligent, well-disciplined
and popular.

That's a bit like the kettle calling the pot black when it comes from
a society rich in bullies and hypocrites.

If you want to win *Celebrity in the Jungle* here is what you need to do:

• appear all shy and sweet: never criticize a fellow camp-mate, and keep
clutching a cuddly toy as if it were your missing progeny (doesn't always)

• keep your friends in the studio even sweeter if you want to get their votes

• cry as often as you can/laugh like you are a bit simple and not a threat

• make up stories about your past to gain plenty of sympathy

• speak in a soft and endearing way while at the same time planning
where to stand your trophy

• appear innocent and slightly stupid/don't be ugly

• NEVER EAT TOO MUCH SPICY FOOD; IT WILL RUIN YOUR COMPLEXION.

Dennis Wise was an outstanding footballer who had to show strength
and leadership to beat his opponents. Being small meant he had to
stand up to people a lot bigger than himself, especially the one's
from privileged backgrounds born with a silver spoon in their gobs*
Not once did he shirk from a task or whinge he wasn't feeling up to it.
*Always remember: the truth is what the strong say it is.

Best Christmas quote from 'Ben Hur:'
"Look for them in the valley of the lepers......if you can still recognize them!"

Assassination always a possibility

By HERPES ZOSTER | Published: DECEMBER 9, 2017 | Edit

In Roman times it was commonplace to replace an Emperor if you didn't like the way they were
doing things, or they were utterly fking useless.
Stalin didn't ask if he was doing the right thing when he heard
that someone didn't like him and therefore ordered an execution.
There was no: 'aggression is wrong,' so we will re-name it 'being
assertive.' They just got on with the task in hand. Authority
was the one with the biggest sword. The very same Authority
which said that aggression was wrong, and defiance was wrong.

THESE DAYS WE AREN'T EVEN ALLOWED TO CARRY A STILETTO WITHOUT IT
GETTING ALL OVER THE NEWS.

Peace and joy to the world!

Police working on cameras that will see into your living room or up your ass
By BIRD DUNG | Published: DECEMBER 1, 2017 | Edit

Anyone using a computer or laptop need to be vigilant.
It's only a matter of time before these devices are up and running!

Comments

Self-fulfilling prophecy

By HERPES ZOSTER | Published: DECEMBER 7, 2017 | Edit

My partner said she could sense that her Christmas this year was going to be a bad one.
As predicted, her son tried to get her to travel across many miles in the snow. X-box one! She's a pensioner.
After eight hours of repetitive parrot moaning I said;
"How would you like to spend Christmas on your own? Change the record!"
"Alright, I will do."

Deacon Jack

By HERPES ZOSTER | Published: DECEMBER 7, 2017 | Edit
Church attendance has been falling for a number of years, but this week has bucked the trend. Right Reverend Canon Andrew Beane (no relation):

"Good morning Christine. This is the third time we have seen you today..."

Anyone expecting another sprog, like the new Deacon, is bound to get her attention.

She likes babies. I've often seen flies attracted by the smelliest piece of ....

Labels work so well

- *They'll* get a good job and *you won't*, no matter how hard you try
- They will live in luxury, while you could be out on the street
- Their kids will go to public school, while you'll be lucky if you have any
- They will be looked on with admiration and affection, while you could be fortunate to have two half-pennies to rub together
- They will live into a ripe old age, while you will be shunned wherever you go
- They will talk about equality, but will believe they are superior, even among their friends

*Labels! Why they work so well in a competitive society.

HIGHLY RESPECTED SCREWS

By GODFREY WINKLEBACKER | Published: DECEMBER 1, 2017 | Edit

I attended the University Hospital yesterday to see about a knee replacement.

We went to sit down in the queue outside Radiology. Connie Church-Committee was there. She's a friend of Margaret's. I wasn't too surprised to see Lucifer Lawrence handing out his business cards. He was wearing a nice tweed jacket and his customary bow-tie.

After a while a group of men came round the corner. I saw Lawrence instinctively whisper to the Connie woman. They both got up and retreated to a far corner...

One of the men was in handcuffs. The other two looked fat and arrogant. They wore the black uniform of prison guards. The man sat down in the middle. I could feel the atmosphere grow extremely fearful.

"Look at the mean spiteful face," one woman said. "He must have done something really wicked. He might even be a child-killer."

The in-mate had extremely thick wavy hair. His eyes were small and fish-like. He looked like an old piece of chalk and had a huge scar across one cheek. A paper-thin moustache on his upper lip. His trousers were hanging down, nearly falling off. He didn't look at anyone, but was reading a book by Michel Foucault. One of the women complained about him being able to bring a book in with him.

When I came back from the canteen I handed him a cup of tea with some milk and sugar. I also gave him a Kit-Kat.

I went over to sit down. When I looked back one of the guards was eating the Kit-Kat, and the other was stirring the cup of tea.

Supermarket Melon head

By GODFREY WINKLEBACKER | Published: DECEMBER 1, 2017 | Edit

Saw an Officer swanking off at the Tesco Customer Service desk this morning.
"Here to ask for your old job back?" I asked. *Comments*

Hard-core porn found on all police computers

By GODFREY WINKLEBACKER | Published: DECEMBER 1, 2017 | Edit

I dare say it's been there for years.

Purely for 'educational purposes.'

Some people have nothing better to do.

'Just doing our job for the good of you all.'

Hands *above* the desk Sergeant! *Comments*

Now it's official!

By RUMPLESTILTSKIN | Published: NOVEMBER 29, 2017

1 Paying for sex is the same as *rape*.
2 It's okay for women to grope men.
3 My name's Ugly Doris. I'd give anything for Todd Grimshaw to have a feel of me.

Former soldiers released from jail for gun smuggling

By USULI TWELVES | Published: NOVEMBER 27, 2017 | Edit

British soldiers accused of carrying guns 'for their own protection' have been released from a rat-infested prison cell in Asia.
It just goes to show:
Another Judge, another day…
Does anyone believe a single shred of this crap?
The GOOD NEWS! Prince Harry is to marry *into* Hollywood!

Malicious premeditated Government attack on You-tube

By USULI TWELVES | Published: NOVEMBER 25, 2017 | Edit

I've been expecting this for quite a while. The Government, and its Authorities, do not like anything which is not under their control. 'Control' being the operative word here.

A State obsessed with controlling its subjects will do anything within its power to curtail free-speech, liberty and self-determination.

The first excuse is usually 'terrorism.' That's not State-terrorism by the way, but any kind of creed which presents a different perspective on the world to theirs and which doesn't exist within its domain. Any opinion different to theirs will be labelled as dangerous, subversive or immoral. This has been going on since the dawn of time. The Establishment accuses the organisation it wants to bring down of either sponsoring terrorism, or of having some kind of responsibility for its existence.

The second excuse is usually that the organisation is somehow responsible for the abuse of children. Anyone dense, on hearing that accusation, will react with horror and revulsion, without questioning their motive more thoroughly. The Government know (like any vindictive partner) that an accusation of this nature will DESTROY the object of their attack. I have not seen any of the actual comments concerned, but would not be at all surprised if some of them were found to be made by people working for the Authorities themselves. As easy as, say, planting DNA at the scene of a crime when the alleged perpetrator is a member of the Roman Catholic clergy. I would hazard a guess that the alleged comments were not all meant to be taken seriously, but were someone's idea of a sick joke.

Still, when you are working for the Authorities, or the Government, and you have an agenda, such as a dislike of videos posted by the General Public you don't approve of, or which are critical of you, what other option do you have?

There will always be members of the herd willing to stampede on your behalf.

Don't let Andrew get the car!

By PETER SMITH | Published: DECEMBER 4, 2017 | Edit

Called past the garage today. Jeremy was lurking outside. He's the Owner.
He told me that my mum and sister had been up a while back
to ask him to keep the car with him.
"We don't want Andrew to get the car!"
"But mum told me she was going to give me the car?!!"
"Bitches!"
He told me that she had given the car to him for him to use.
"Don't worry," he said. "I won't say anything. Women are a funny lot!" You're telling me.

Grossly offensive Maynard

By GODFREY WINKLEBACKER | Published: NOVEMBER 22, 2017 |

After only two days in the celebrity jungle little Jack Maynard is being forced to leave 'by common consent,' and it hasn't got anything to do with full-frontals posted on-line. Tipped as a possible winner we weren't even allowed to get to know him properly so we could judge for ourselves.

Months ago, on his hugely popular vlog, he had used *incorrect and inappropriate language*, which his growing army of fans were only too delighted to applaud.

FUCKWIT

PAIR OF RETARDS

CHIMNEY-SWEEP

I wonder who snitched this time? I'm sure another ambitious wanna-be will replace him soon. Just as long as they have the right connections and are not averse to a large financial reward.

*Thankfully, we have an Establishment only too willing to watch over us and to protect us from abusive and offensive posts.

It's alright to take the piss out of some people, but not others!

POST OFFICE PLEBS

By RUMPLESTILTSKIN | Published: NOVEMBER 21, 2017 | Edit

Called in our only Post Office yesterday to send in some new material to the British Library.

"'Are they on a go-slow again?"

"They're doing the best they can," said a woman ahead of me turning around.

"How *do you* know?"

I handed my envelopes to the Assistant.

"I'd prefer them 'un-opened' today."

The Assistant went several shades of purple and replied:

"I never open the mail. It's against the law."

"Look, I'm not a simpleton," I said. "I know that under certain circumstances they do! I like to walk round with my eyes open myself."

She looked at me as if she wanted the earth to swallow me up.

"And another thing," I said. "How about a chair at the side of the queue. It takes hours to get served here sometimes. I'm only thinking of the old aged pensioners. But then, I'm only a customer."

One of the people in the queue laughed.

"There's a chair at the office table, oh alright. I will put it in our suggestion box."

Crazy Teacher

By BIRD DUNG | Published: NOVEMBER 18, 2017 | Edit

I visited the library Wednesday. As our local pariah, I was unaccompanied.
A member of the NUT was sitting on her chair. It was quite a shock: the *gossip around town* suggested she had even been too afraid to look out from behind one her own curtains. I pretended I hadn't seen her. I don't think I've ever seen anyone put on their hat and coat so quick, or scoot out of the exit. I have no idea why she would want to surreptitiously surf the net away from home, unless she had something to hide of course... It wasn't long ago that I was receiving gifts on my birthday and at Christmas. Now, zilch! All because I confessed to having a past and had asked someone: 'if her husband smiled would his face cave in...?'
The last time I saw Brian's head spinning round while reciting the Lord's prayer backwards I decided not to keep going to their church. It was all a bloody sham anyway. Guess I just wasn't freaky enough. Most of the congregation appeared dead from the neck up and the doorman always seemed to be suffering from cramp in his neck.
Most likely, she was scurrying back to tell 'Lucifer' Lawrence that she had seen me. He's a strange fish. Someone in our town told someone else to tell someone that someone he knew had said he liked to use a mirror to look up their skirts in his revolving chair.

Cheesus loves you!

You're not having her!

By HERPES ZOSTER | Published: NOVEMBER 17, 2017 | Edit

Yvonne rang this morning to bark down the phone.
Brian was busy fighting on his X-box.
A letter from the Benefits office still lay on the doormat.
"Wherever Sophia goes, I go!" she shouted.
She's starting school next September?
"*And* you called me a big fat lazy cow!"

Mum's lost all her marbles

By HERPES ZOSTER | Published: NOVEMBER 17, 2017 | Edit

Mum tried to raid my room at five in the morning last night but was unable to get through the second barricade.
"What have you done with my medical file?" she railed.
"I'm going to have you locked up in prison if I can't find it soon.!"

The return of Corrie's Robert

By GODFREY WINKLEBACKER | Published: NOVEMBER 14, 2017 | Edit

Coronation Street's Robert returned from prison last night and took up where his life had left off:

A close loving relationship
A supportive and faithful partner
A successful business, thriving, with lots of happy customers
A crowd of cheering friends and allies
A benevolent and forgiving Establishment
A nice comfortable home
A pat on the back from the Authorities
A healthy complexion, strong and sun-tanned

*Just like real life then!

OLD SOLDIERS NEVER DIE, THEY SIMPLY FADE AWAY!

Why should a cunt like Piers Morgan be allowed to interview poor people accused of being serial killers?

Lucifer Lawrence

By GODFREY WINKLEBACKER | Published: DECEMBER 17, 2017 | Edit

I've had that Count Lawrence sniffing up my back-side for a few weeks now and spreading malicious rumours. I'm really getting hacked off with him stalking me all the time. Can't he find anyone else to bullshit to? If it wasn't for him there would be no dangerous dogs in the village. He's one of those slippery characters who is always nice to your face and planning your execution as soon as your back is turned.

Oh, I nearly forgot: he's born again and has more than a hundred grandchildren.

Gen's got the car!

By RUMPLESTILTSKIN | Published: DECEMBER 30, 2017 | Edit

My sister ordered the car to be brought back from the car mechanic yesterday. I am to be allowed to drive it again!

The Target Practice

By GODFREY WINKLEBACKER | Published: DECEMBER 29, 2017 |
WE AIM TO PROVIDE THE MOST PROFESSIONAL, IMPARTIAL
AND CONFIDENTIAL SERVICE POSSIBLE:

covert surveillance only when you ask
a friendly team of Carers able to cater for your every need
nice warm surroundings with plenty of free magazines to read
regular briefings with our local constabulary

Andrew Marr

By HERPES ZOSTER | Published: DECEMBER 25, 2017 | Edit
Utterly fking useless

A complete face-ache

Unable to form joined-up sentences

Member of the old school tie

Still in with the Gaffers

A string on his violin broke

Celebrity Big Brother

By RUMPLESTILTSKIN | Published: JANUARY 6, 2018 | Edit

Celebrity Big Brother is a true representation of the people living in our society. Ann Widdecombe looks a bit lost in there at the moment. One of the trannies went to the diary room to say she was a: "miserable old woman with a face like a bag of spanners!""She called me a man! I'm not going to let her forget it."

Tonight, we were treated to the arrival of 'Twinkletoes,' the dancing dwarf, who seems to be getting everywhere at the moment, and a man dressed as a woman who deliberately dropped his dress on entering the house just so we were in no doubt about his gender. What a bunch of twats.

We are supposed to respect everyone in our society and treat them equally. Who is responsible for spreading this trash?

Shades of Grey

By RUMPLESTILTSKIN | Published: DECEMBER 30, 2017 | Edit

Always get your own way if you are sexy and good looking
pretend to be one of the elite
Don't give a damn about anyone else
Dominate men and women alike because you are richer than them
Get angry and throw things around if they don't do as they're told
Behave aggressively and abusively towards others
Fuck hard and let them know it
Become admired and desired by everyone who sees you
*No wonder he's so popular with women across the planet

Comrade Lenin

By BIRD DUNG | Published: JANUARY 11, 2018 | Edit

During the First World War comrade Lenin was given free passage through Europe by the Germans. They thought that his presence in Russia would prevent their greatest enemy from taking any further part in the conflict, which it did. The only thing he wasn't given was free-speech. He was kept safely trapped inside his railway compartment with guards stationed on either side of his door in case he spoke to anyone and triggered a revolution.

A WAR-TIME ROMANCE

Shrinkage due to age

By BIRD DUNG | Published: JANUARY 11, 2018 | Edit

It's well known that as we age we also shrink. Everything becomes smaller including our I.Q. Some of us have more to lose than others. I, for instance, used to be about six foot four, but I have slowly decreased in height since my late teens. I'm a bit worried about my cock as well.

Joined a Dating agency

By GODFREY WINKLEBACKER | Published: DECEMBER 18, 2017 | Edit

Before I meet anyone I need to re-order some more rope and make sure my axe is nicely sharpened

The disfiguring of body parts

By PETER SMITH | Published: JANUARY 12, 2018 | Edit

For a fair number of years now I have worked at one of the top transplant clinics in the world performing many difficult operations. Because I want to go down in the annals of history as one of the best doctors in my field I have taken to scribbling my moniker on whatever is being put in. It's just a little quirk I have. It's not meant to hurt anyone. You get more blood shaving in a morning and the patient doesn't feel a frigging thing. I usually carve my initials S J (Sir John) or C P S (Counts and Piss-takers). Some people may think I am abusing my trust, but look at the way the Government is ruining the cpuntry. I carry out my vocation with the minimum of fuss. It does not impair my confidence in any way. Neither does it cause me any distress. Out with the bad and in with the good I say! You have to watch the buggers in the Health Service. They will do anything to stab you in the back.

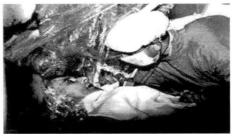

'You appear to have a crack in your franny…!'

WHAT DID THE CHALDEANS DO?

Invented the wheel, calendar, zodiac, war and sublimation, divination, the Hanging gardens of Babylon, and much more...
How come we never learnt about them in school?

I am not a handsome bastard

By RUMPLESTILTSKIN / Published: JANUARY 3, 2018 / Edit

I wish people would stop telling me how good looking I am. It gets very tiring hearing the same monotonous compliments every fking day. I want to be ugly, like Harvey Wine-stain or Julian Lennon. I wish they would leave me alone and go pester someone else! As I've heard many times before; it's not what you look like on the surface its what you are like underneath.

Drain on the National Health Service

By PETER SMITH | *Published: JANUARY 2, 2018* | *Edit*

My girlfriend is convinced that a small spot on her neck is cancer, so she has made an urgent appointment to see the doctor. This is not the first time this has happened, nor is it confined to just one member of her family. She has asked me to pray for her and if I had any expectation about what might be the result. 'They will probably send you down the chemist for a tube of Clearasil,' I answered.

Deafening silence

By HERPES ZOSTER | *Published: JANUARY 11, 2018* | *Edit*

Dear Social Services,

I wrote to you recently about greater co-operation between us all. I am my mother's main carer, and wanted to be included in your meetings about her. So far, I have not received a single reply from mum's Social worker despite several attempts to contact her.

DORCUS

By HERPES ZOSTER | *Published: JANUARY 11, 2018* | *Edit*

Dorcus became very snappy with me last night:
"He is my son!"
"She is my granddaughter!"
"I can do what I like."
"Nobody is forcing me to do anything."
But you said you'd never go there again?
"You don't know what it's like because you've never had any children of your own."

Comments

What's on telly by 'Deafening Silence' Jan 2018

Dorcus: "My dad liked 'Last of the Summer wine.'"
SOP: "I thought you said he didn't drink?"

Dorcus dying from the cold

By GODFREY WINKLEBACKER | *Published: JANUARY 17, 2018* | *Edit*

As reported by other employees of the Bunderchook Estate, Dorcus refused to go and see her son because of the constant insults. She swore she would never go back, not even to hold 'the toy.' On Saturday she travelled all over the city in the cold. Since then she has been slowly dying in agony. I have done all I can to comfort her.

Killed the missus

By HERPES ZOSTER | Published: JANUARY 11, 2018 | Edit

- liked dancing and the taking of prick
- behaved like a tramp whenever you were away
- laughed about you all over the place

Look! If she's like that, why marry her in the first place.
Just leave!

Rizla kids

By HERPES ZOSTER | Published: JANUARY 11, 2018 | Edit

A young shop keeper died because he refused to give three African lads some cigarette papers. Why the frig not? And where are their fathers?

More on the boss/Dear pain-in-the-butt

By HERPES ZOSTER | Published: JANUARY 11, 2018 | Edit

After screaming at my door for forty minutes I gave mum the car keys. She then offered to get me some cut specially for me. She said I was a good son and had a far better nature than Genevieve...

Mum put the keys in the cupboard, but when we looked for them to go to the shop they had disappeared again. She has also taken my book on cats and a cuddly toy from my bathroom. I still haven't got my glasses back yet!

*Drove mum to the church in Holt for the funeral. Empty. Then she said it was at the crematorium, but she didn't know which one or what town it was in. There's no crematorium in Holt. We spent ages driving around and walking in the freezing cold before we went home. I said to her, quite exasperated: "Couldn't you at least have found out where it was before we set off?"

"Oh, shut up!" she said. "You need to lose some weight, you fatty."

Maybe Jenny and Kevin are right. There isn't anything seriously wrong with her and she is perfectly normal.

I'm a good Screw

By GODFREY WINKLEBACKER | Published: JANUARY 17, 2018 | Edit

For the past twenty years I have fulfilled my duty to society:

cared for the sick and needy
fit them up whenever possible
watched them take a shower or peeped through their window
inflicted pain only if it was absolutely necessary
continued to learn my ABC backwards
passed on information to the media for a tidy little sum
held on tightly to my keys
kept in with the gang by regularly bending over the wall
pissed myself whenever we saw Charley come back
told myself time and time again that 'rules must be obeyed!'

Cowardly racist scum

By HERPES ZOSTER | Published: JANUARY 1, 2018 | Edit
It's wrong to compete or to protect one of your own

only bad people call other people names

I'll snitch on you before you do on me

hostility and aggression are a thing of the past

fanatical human beings are worse than animals

it's a sin not to give in to others

Vegans really like meat

By GODFREY WINKLEBACKER | Published: JANUARY 3, 2018 | Edit

For the past nine years I've been working at a Veggie Restaurant in the City. I have regularly left small insects and particles of chicken in their salads. I was so sick of seeing their pasty faces lacking in the right vitamins and minerals. NOTHING ELSE WAS ADDED!

Letter to Mein Fuhrer

By RUMPLESTILTSKIN | Published: JANUARY 13, 2018 | Edit

5th Column,
Old Nancy Street,
Little Delhi.
INDIAN TAKE-AWAY.

Dearest Adolf,

Thank you for your wonderful hospitality when we visited earlier this year. We enjoyed the scenery and our walk about was magnificent. Eva was such pleasant company and not a bit humourless. The uniform fits wonderfully but the iron cross is still a bit heavy. It was great to be treated like royalty once again. I am looking forward to the tanks and being called 'Herr President!' Our kind regards to Joe and his loyal band of heroes. *Georgie-Porgy* cried when mummy got home. Just imagine having a back-stabber for a little brother. And I thought I was a scrawny little wimp. We will send Elizabeth into exile when *we* are through! I tend to think this will not happen immediately but will take some time to accomplish. The wife swapping party could have been better. Charades was super: we just needed a larger elephant. I'm *not mad* at Winston, but he could do with a toupee. We will just have to be careful when entering the Autobahn and look under the car every time we go out. Wallis and I refuse to take part in this game of social hierarchy any more.

Love and Best wishes,
Edward and Wallis

Hatey not a place to practise voodoo or witchcraft

By RUMPLESTILTSKIN | Published: JANUARY 13, 2018 | Edit

If it was there would already be a doll of Donald Trump....

More on Dorcus/stinks of piss (SOP)

By RUMPLESTILTSKIN | Published: JANUARY 13, 2018 | Edit

Dorcus went on a long journey in the cold today. Her son said she could not play with the toy unless she came over for breakfast.
Against all her promises she went.

Nasty Graham Spewels

Graham was a swarthy lad,

Who waited on the homeward path,

For Dorcus on her little bike,

To push her in the stinging nettles.

He laughed and laughed at how,

She cried,

Her skin ablaze with little sores,

but he would never be forgot,

And years thereafter moaned about.

Nothing better than sleeping on the street

By HERPES ZOSTER | Published: DECEMBER 25, 2017 | Edit **If you are a cat.**

COMPETITION

There's nothing better than seeing some poor sod freezing to death at the side of the pavement during winter. It really makes you feel good to see them lying there with the obligatory mangy dog at their feet.   Sleeping rough is something they brought on themselves. The scrounging bastards!

'Gave mum a book about Norfolk and a calendar for Christmas...
She came back from Kevin's delighted,
'did you give me this lovely book...?'
This morning she left it outside my door...
'what a boring book,' she said
'I've never seen one so bland!"

A car

To be frank, I would rather use my mountain bike for everything, but a car can sometimes be useful, especially if you have a girlfriend who cannot walk. Mum had promised me her car for years, when she had finished with it. Today she told me she was giving the cash she received for it to the man who fitted her new boilers.

PROPHETIC DREAM (1980's)

Dear Mr. Archer,

I had a strange dream about you last night. I dreamt that you sent me a cheque for £50,000. I have no idea why you should have encroached into my thoughts while I was asleep. I hope you don't mind me writing to tell you about it.

SEPARATE BEDS

Geraldine and Brian have had separate beds since they married. That was forty years ago. He's not allowed to touch her. Especially with his cock. They don't have any children except for 'Christine.'

CHEWING GUM

I told Henry to pick her up outside the school-yard at half past four. Then he was to drive along the main High-street. He would instruct Jessica to call in the newsagents. As she was returning he would drag her into his car and drive off at great speed, making sure everyone in town could hear her screaming through the window. Henry would meet us at the derelict cottage on the moor. It stood beside a small group of trees and inside an old stone yard. He was to leave his mobile phone switched on and turn on his transistor radio. The van was to be left outside in the open, with a pair of white knickers thrown carelessly on a slab nearby. After that they were to enter through the front door and lock it. The secret passage under the stairs would bring them safely back to town.

Then leave the rest to us...

'The Warlord weaves his web of fear,

Each man receives his fated share,

A blood-red sun is the Warrior's wield,

The eagle scans the battlefield.'

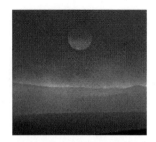

Inimicus humanae naturae

So, you think that I am mentally deranged,

And all my scattered verbiage to decay,

That all my valiant efforts were in vain,

To see beneath your skin of meretricious lies.

For mind is grizzled with a sea of pearls,

Exploding variables of living fire,

Among these gems of Universe, I hiss,

The staff of life into a Spoiler's breath.

Under the morning cloud I hold my knife,

A rampant wolf, with teeth of grinding ice,

My furious longing twisted into rope,

With which to hang you from horizon's eyes.

By your decay, does my abundance grow,

Beneath the vibrant whirring of the glows,

Dividing flame, I clap, and raise my arms,

And bring this tearful conflict to a final close.

A flood will I become,

And rivers wild,

Burning fields of pestilence and plague,

The land-bound comet into your lap,

Submerge the features of this loving world.

Landru (Nov 1983)

ESCAPE

I first met Dorothy on my walk up the hill to the bus-stop during my days as chief bottom wiper and games technician in the Health Service.

It was on those sunny days at the side of the park where we used to stop and chat that I first glimpsed what beautiful blue eyes she had. A sort of cross, between Gracie Fields and Hannah Hawkswell I mused. She had a faintly sensitive, fragile voice.

I would see her coming towards me in the distance with her grey hair wrapped up into a bun. It took me months to invite her over for coffee. I don't know what I intended to do with her, but I'm sure I would have thought of something.

At seventy years old she was fifty years older than me, but it hardly seemed to matter. She seemed to have such a lovely character.

I heard a light knock on my door one day, but by the time I got there whoever it was had gone. She told me a week later that she had been round to see me. I was surprised.

I didn't see her for a long time. She seemed more forgetful. Less together.

One day I called a builder in to do some work for me. I was shocked to learn that he was her son and that she had about eight children, including him.

I'm an old man myself now, so why should her face and voice suddenly appear again in my thoughts?

On Saturday it was freezing cold, but I had made up my mind to take the plates across, no matter how far it was, or how ill I was feeling.

I managed to get to Reepham alright, but then I had to ask directions. A local man advised me to take the path along Marriot's way through the woods.

It was 'only a mile,' he said.

I wish I hadn't bothered. The track was covered in hawthorns.

By the time I found the house the sun was already sinking in the sky, and clouds were beginning to darken the road. There was a red glow over the horizon as I eventually entered her drive and cycled up towards Primrose Farm. I went to the wrong door at first. The cottage was overgrown with brambles, and there didn't seem anyone in. Eventually I saw someone drifting to the front door. It opened, and a bent-over, grey-haired lady, beckoned me in.

"I have never seen a place like it!" I said.

"I like hoarding things!" she said.

Her cottage was crammed with boxes full to bursting.

I unpacked my plates. I thought they had come from Larner's, but she told me they were from 'Jarrold's.' The lady went to make me a cup of tea and offered me some rich tea biscuits. She pulled out a chair for me to sit on.

"I'm wasn't sure how old you were," she said.

"I'm sorry I can't stop long. I'll have to go back before it gets too dark."

"Look at how big your hands are. You have got beautiful skin for eighty-six."

She said that her husband was like a baby for the last two years of his life. That she too had been ill with cancer. That's why she wore a large blue bow over her head.

"You know how to tell if someone's poorly? Stick out your tongue! You are as healthy as anything. There's not a thing wrong with you," I laughed.

The lady had piercing blue eyes and a sharp wit. She said her daughter sometimes came to take her shopping.

She reached into her bag and give me four pounds for coming. That made fourteen pounds in all.

Before I left I embraced her and she kissed me. It felt sweet, as if she loved me.

GIANT

I first met the Giant, Thomas Cahill, in 1967. To me he was a giant. To you he was probably of normal height. I came from a family of dwarfs, elves and pixies. My Gran said I was telling fairy stories when I told her how big he was. He had reddish brown hair, a strong chin and nose. He had a pale skin, with a calming presence. That didn't prevent me from doing the two-hand challenge when we met. We were in Miss McNulty's class; he bent my hands right back. I'd never been beaten before. He didn't really want to have a trial of strength, but I felt it was my duty to challenge him because of his size. It hurt my wrists, but I decided I would have another go at him another day.

At twelve years old Thomas was already shagging the girls from Peter Black's. I was still running around in short trousers and playing tiddlywinks.

I followed Thomas around for quite a while, hoping that some of his height might rub off on me. At thirteen we went to the Grammar School. Once again, he was put in the same class as me. He sat beside me throughout the next four years. I even had him in my maths' class. He was the only one who could teach me anything.

I saw Sabelli hit him on the football pitch one day. Thomas squared up to him and retaliated. It shocked me. There was only ever going to be one winner. He was normally such a gentleman.

He was a fantastic runner, but he still couldn't beat Sean Butler, who was Yorkshire champion at the time. I watched him do his hardest to win at our annual school games, sprinting like a lion down the track. Danny O'Hara came in a close third.

The only time I ever saw Thomas blush, was when we found out that his father was a pig-farmer. If we ever wanted to embarrass him from that moment on all we had to do was mention his dad.

When we were sixteen we went on a pub crawl through some of the small villages in the Craven District. We were all drunk by the time we entered Sutton Town Hall. It was packed to bursting with head-swinging rockers. As our small band of inebriates made it to the centre of the dance hall a slurry of lads seemed to emerge from every direction. It was almost too dark to see who was there. The biggest of them, though dwarfed by our Thomas, confronted him in the middle of the floor, with the rest of the mob egging him on. Then all hell seemed to break loose. That's the last thing I saw before we all bolted out of the door and down the steps to safety. Thomas appeared outside the hall about twenty minutes later with his hair slightly ruffled and not one of the gang left standing.

*In memory of my friend Thomas Cahill, who passed away at the age of only fifty.

Further discussions with the Plebs

1 Why do you keep asking me what time I get up?

2 Two cases dropped in the same number of days because you didn't give the Defence lawyers all the information you had. How many years have you been able to get away with that?

3 I feel a bit like Alfred Itch-cock with my camera recording your on-going harassment. It's okay. I will only record you from the neck down. Wouldn't want to damage my lens.

4 What's a Sex pest?

5 Don't say I told you, but I think Mat's a bit of a 'wrong 'un.'

6 Morph? Yes, my camera is still rolling.

7 I'm only trying to help you.

8 Why am I on the Register?

9 Ten years ago I contacted an ex-partner on the phone. Someone I didn't want even when we slept in the same bed. I was charged with breaking a restraining order not to contact her (one landline call where I said I was sorry about a misunderstanding and that I never intended to hurt her and <u>one</u> disputed text message). It was not malicious or threatening. Here's a copy of the actual charge. Any mention of that dirty word 'sex' in there?

10 Close to the end of my sentence for the phone contact you applied for a SOPO order claiming I was going to commit a serious sexual offence such as rape against my ex or a member of the public. Something I would never do. I was never charged with any kind of sexual offence against my partner. On the SOPO you claimed I was a threat to her and the children. When I asked why they were named on the order the only excuse you could come up with was that her son had seen me locking the downstairs door from the top of the stairs one evening. What's dangerous about that? It was just an excuse to 'keep tabs on me.' As a biproduct of getting the order you were able to put me on the Sex Offender's Register. That's the only way you could keep coming round to harass me.

11 Is your excuse anything to do with there being 'too much digital information for you to cope with?' You banned me from the library.

12 Being naked is not a sexual offence. There was no sexual activity. I was simply seen half naked through a changing room curtain while getting changed in a clothes' shop. Myself and my partner see it every day and it's never offended us. That was years ago.

13 Do ex partner's ever lie about withholding personal possessions belonging to you. Do you think they ever lie about anything else, especially with a financial incentive, such as making up stories about you sending *numerous* messages?

14 What do you think of labels for pots of jam?

15 Have you cuffed anyone today?

16 Did you do much report writing in the army. How are you at taking orders? Please, just GO!

17 Cor, blimey! Is that the time.

18 Did you ever want to be famous?

19 Why don't you stick your next assessment where the squirrel stuck it's nuts.

20 How many gay Managers do you work for?

21 Do you know your colleague Sarah Watergate? Nice legs. Could have sworn I saw her in a lap-dancing club once.

22 Do you ever see Aaron. I hear he's very popular in the States. I thought I saw his name on the side of a loaf of bread, but when I looked more closely it said 'THICK CUT.'

23 Why did you have to clone my computer. Don't you have enough clones already in the staff room?

24 Do you think we live in a more tolerant society?

MUPPET!

Pigs need shit like horses need a blanket.

I've been asked to provide more intense lashings from my acidic tongue for you to froth over. Some of my readers have been moaning about my lack of true venom, especially Father Christmas and his band of sycophants. DNA always available!

WARNING!

You are being watched by all the staff in this library.

The truth about 'Mare:' He's gay!

 **REVIEW**

A great book to take on holiday if you ever need ...

By Amazon Customer on 18 December 2017

A great book to take on holiday if you ever need a small amount of fuel to make a camp fire. Proof that Mr Lawrence's wit and flair for the obscure have not been dulled by his retirement. For the price of about seventy cans of dog food you can send yourself to sleep with a clear conscience. I am sure this work will be hailed by Born again egg-heads everywhere as the greatest contribution to literature since the gospels but for me it didn't really hit the Mark. For those who know Mr Lawrence personally his charm and lip-drooping after dinner hogwash could easily be mistaken for Bond himself...

 **CHRISTMAS CARD MESSAGE**

'To my gorgeous beautiful lovely sister Margaret, at Christmas,

From her equally gorgeous and lovely brother at home in slum-town.

What a wonderful charming family we all are!' XXX

Oh, dear! There I go: encouraging violence and public unrest again...

'You certainly don't mince words, but that's fine. I do agree that violence begets violence: it doesn't make the world safer. May I add that, reading your posts, I sense a deep anger and your wish to change the world. All of this is admirable. We need people who dare speak in uncertain terms. For my own part, I probably tend to choose other words, but that's my right. I too want a just world and fight for it in my way and with my own words (if you can own words: I'm not sure). I have a question for you though: why do you present yourself as POET?'

Hanne Holte

Gypsy Christmas

Mammy sat with baby Kate,

A bottle warming on the grate.

About our Christmas feast,

We sang,

With Terry on the telly.

Daddy bought for Uncle Keith,

A big horse with damn awful teeth,

Eileen came to open toys,

I smiled at Jane, expecting now.

Brian with an open book,

Granny dishing out the sprouts,

And Jimmy showing us his bike.

Grandad poured a slug for Tommy...

In a special glass we drank,

Around the candelabra danced,

Our brown donkey was inside,

Making lots of jelly.

Yet while we played the angels heard,

Before paying our annual call,

To hang our graves with flowers and rhymes.

Pictures of those who'd gone away.

We heard a bark in our back yard,

The twisting of the iron gate,

The yell of people in the street,

Billy ran and bit a leg.

By the holly, with her Mick,

Eileen lay her fiddle stick,

Mammy raised her pallid head,

At noises from the winter.

We heard the crack of gunfire sound,

Bottles fell and bottles cloud,

As Council men turned up our home,

Their bellies fat with beer and balm.

The Digger ate into our wall,

And shouting came from other falls:

"Get outta here y' dirty twats!"

"We don't want you in our town!"

"You came down here without permission!"

The policemen leered at our small children.

Other families fought and spat,

But there was only one that night,

With bloody eyes and Santa's sack,

Ready to meet the devil.

Brother Jim was in handcuffs,

His head was cut and so was mine,

We stumbled in the darkened lane,

In nothing but our bare feet.

A loud crescendo reached our lugs,

Cheering came from good townsfolk,

The Vicar with his new prayer-book,

Copters tracked us up the road...

With burly Coppers laughing loud,

The water pipes were broke and cracked.

Prematurely aged and bound,

The big-time man with swollen knees,

The Neddies dragged and tow-bars tugged,

The time for explanations gone...

Beg your food and bet your mam,

Not wanted anywhere it seems:

"I'm not telling you the Status quo!"

"Arrested for your own safety!"

"The only benefit is yours.!"

"Force if only necessary!"

"Obstruct us at your jeopardy!"

"We don't want you Irish here!"

"Gone within a fucking hour!"

I can't read or write milord...

Bursting with indignant fire.

An apron wise, an apron stiff.

The Coppers were almost in bliss.

Left us in the bloody wind.

We began our walk again,

Our shameful mien our sorry den,

Through hillock, field and muddy lane,

To meet our folk across the sea,

To stand amidst the Gypsy Trees.

Don't believe all you hear. Better to hear it from the horse's mouth...!
(Facebook comment on hearing someone has being spreading malicious gossip around all my friends).
NATIONAL HEALTH SERVICE BANKRUPTING THE COUNTRY

VAMPIRE

<u>Andrew "Andy" Gallagher</u> was one of the Special Children who had the psychic power of mind control and through training and meditation developed the ability of *mental projection.*

Early Life

Andy's mother Holly Beckett was pregnant with him and his twin brother at the age of 18, but gave them up and they both were adopted by different families. Andy's adopted mother was murdered by the demon Azazel above Andy's crib when he was six months old, but Webber's adopted mother was not.

I suppose I have President Bill Clinton to thank for this. **Not often you have a vampire named after you!**

Andy pick-pocket

AeroFlight

AeroFlight

Name:
Carole Taggart
Boarding time: To: **Los Angeles**
5th April
2018 SEAT
22J

I have been in touch with the Cops there and have given them a full description, including your seat number and flight. They have assured me that you will be breaking the law if you try to jump from the Bridge and that they will be waiting for you when you arrive...Carole Taggart shared a **link**.

2 January at 22:10 ·

Where Will You Travel In 2018?

According to your taste!

WEARETESTS.COM

Ode to the trooper

Oh, Peter Manion, you are great,
We could put you in a crate,
Keep you till your legs were long,
Or you had a different dong.

Your dada was a dick like you,
Your mam was simple,
That was true,
Your sister covered for your crimes,
And lit the fag up on your grave.

BUNTING FAR BY Crowmarsh Gifford

THE WEDDING FEAST AT CANAAN (OR

'MY SECRET JOURNEY INTO MADNESS')

I'm going to try and work a bloody miracle; I'm going to try to make sense of everything that's happened. Not just for you, but for me as well.

There are things which should have been said a long time ago but weren't. Things which were said which shouldn't have been. Nothing I say is meant to embarrass you in any way, but I will have to mention everything which I think is relevant. I just need you to understand the truth and not what people who don't know me have said about me. In all the time I knew you did I ever do anything deliberately to hurt you?

I know you tried to ring me several times, but I just couldn't pick up the phone. I'm not sure why. I never found it easy to talk to you. It just seemed easier to keep you in suspense.

I once gave you a piece of paper with ten things I wanted to discuss with you written down. When I came back from the kitchen it was tossed down the side of the sofa. You said you had read it, but you said nothing. Words are important to me. I prefer to express myself through words.

Some of what you read may be a bit distressing. I am sorry about that, but I just want you to understand what you have done, and why I did what I did. Some things are very hard to talk about...as time's gone on you must have done a lot of things I haven't been a part of, but there are many questions which still need to be answered. Trying to make sense of the terrible sequence of events may actually make them more

bearable. Surely all this suffering can't have been for nothing...?
I may have strained the boundaries somewhat, and I do tend to challenge
authority, but I have never been an unpleasant or malicious person. Most things
have been as a result of my mischievous nature, my habit of taking risks, my
temptation to bend the rules, and to question everything.
I can't begin to say how sorry I am about how events have turned out. I am truly
sorry for all the hurt and upheaval I have caused you, but you can't go through
the rest of your life believing what is wrong about me. I'm not perfect.

I know I have a devilish streak, and I have done a lot of things I haven't been
proud of, but you only have to scratch the surface to find your *Guardian angel*.
There are lots of things I would change if I could do.
When I met you I never wanted you to think I was anything other than a decent
caring thoughtful gentleman.
Please read carefully what I have to say in private, quietly, without any
interference from anyone else.
When we first met you seemed very vulnerable and withdrawn. I drove across in
the work van and kissed you through the window (your cheek was very soft). I
recognised your voice from the phone. You were saying goodnight to some
Solicitor friends. I couldn't stay very long. It was already dark.
You complained later about the times I came over. It was quieter in the evenings at
work and it was the only time I could really get away.

Another reason is because I find it a lot more peaceful and relaxing after the sun
has gone down and when there aren't a lot of people around.
I contacted you because you lived close by and I felt like some fresh company.

You seemed a bit straight up and down. Not very curvy.

You were very different to anyone I had ever known before.
The second time we met you invited me in and we cuddled on the sofa. You sent me a
message on my way across which read... *'in lust...something something:'* I thought it was
a bit inappropriate. I wasn't really looking for that. Your skin wasn't like anything I had
ever felt before.
You made me a fish curry which was actually very nice even though you refused to
believe it but I didn't like you forcing my hand to make you climax.
You made it very obvious what you were looking for and I felt it was my obligation to
oblige, but I didn't enjoy any of it. You made me suck your breasts to see if they were still
providing milk. Emily was six, so you would have had to be doing something unusual for
them to go on producing for so long. Anyway, I went along with the occasion, but it all

seemed a bit crazy. You said that you thought Brian had left you because your tummy was too fat. It wasn't that. You said that you never felt really confident about yourself, so I tried to rebuild your confidence as best I could.

There was nothing I didn't like about you physically, and you did have blue eyes, but there was nothing I felt particularly attracted to either. You seemed very fragile. You asked me several times: "do you think you could love me, just a little bit?" I felt a bit unsure because I didn't know you. You seemed alright.

I thought you had a lovely home, and it was in a nice part of the country. You seemed to have all the material things in life but very little direction.

You acted as muddled as a hen at a foxhunt. One minute you were a drab housewife, next minute 'Mother Theresa,' and then a 'craving nymphomaniac.' I wasn't sure what I was doing there or what I really wanted from you, if anything. You said that when you came back from Saudi and were living in London you were quite promiscuous and only used men for sex (but not that many!). I tried to make excuses for your conflicting changes of opinion by saying you were trying to view life from a number of different angles, but I disagreed with you about how you went about things. I decided you were totally wrong for me, but that it didn't really matter because I was never going to stay with you. I told myself that I should never get involved with your family and that they were incongruous and always bickering.

There is a reason why I never intended to stay which I would like to tell you about... You asked me if we got along and I said yes. I decided then that I could always come back to you whatever happened; it was your vulnerability and craziness...your acceptance, and your gregarious nature.

I went to bed with you without any real desire at all; because you seemed to want me there. You gave me one of Brian's t-shirts to wear.

You turned up at my place of work early in the morning and shoved a card through the letterbox. It was pink and very sweet. You woke me up.

You used to ask me where I was: all-the-time. You sometimes pleaded with me to let you drive across and stay the night. You seemed desperate not to be left on your own. When I rang you from work it was quite funny: "two minutes" – you'd disappear, and all I could hear for ages was shouting while you put the kids to bed. You put a lot of pressure on me which I wasn't really prepared for, but I continued to come round to see you, even though I never felt really sure about my intentions. I am a very quiet person in spite of my outward appearance, and I'm very shy sometimes. I don't like a lot of people around.

About three weeks after we had started sleeping together I went to Wales with my employers. You tried to speak to me every single night. Rose once said to me that she didn't know how you managed to hold down your job sometimes. You were reprimanded for not taking enough time with a patient and for doing your shopping in work time. Rose once asked me if you were still drinking and where you were hiding all the bottles. I should have been more understanding. I should have been more sympathetic about what you had been through and the stresses on your life. We both agreed that all we wanted was for you to be happy. I should have been more loving. Rose said that she and Dennis had been intervening in your marriage and helping to heal the arguments for the final four years. On the night Brian restrained you and you called the police to have him arrested he said: "there's no way I'm putting this in there!" No wonder he didn't come back for six weeks. You said that the reason it had lasted so long was because the sexual side had always worked...sharing confidences and making disclosures to each other is very important too. For a long time you hid your married name from me, which was: 'Strange.'

I tried to help you but I didn't want to touch you. I don't really know why. I am very sensitive to location and to the situation I'm in.

I once went through your entire wardrobe and drawers. I read everything I could in an effort to understand where I was. It was in the days you left me at home. I never saw you wearing anything sexy or seductive.

I watched you go and pay for the petrol in Benson once and watched you walk back again. I couldn't see a single thing I desired, which is very regrettable.

Do you remember the flies that summer? They were everywhere. On the ceiling, in the bedroom, on the fly paper. I cleaned the house several times and hoovered them up in thousands from the floor. The paper said it was the farm nearby.

We went along to church together for weeks and I met all your friends, even though I had rejected standard Christianity long ago. Then you said you wouldn't go if I was going. Apparently, people were asking why we weren't married.

It was a taste of normal family life I had never had. It was sweet to see the children attending their little groups. I suppose it must have happened to me once-upon-a -time. I went to pick you up at a nearby Garden party. I was a bit late. You cried and ran to me. The first time I started thinking about you was after seeing you trying to play the violin in church. It was hilarious. Very brave!

I remember you calling a dinner party. You invited a lot of your old friends including Justine. She told you that she thought I was very well groomed.

 I wasn't really in the mood for socialising but I tried my best for you. They were all nice people and very respectable. Your behaviour was a bit erratic though.

Later in the evening as we were at the table I stood up. It was quite mellow in the candlelight. (I sometimes cooked you a meal, especially if I was off work, for you to come home to). You suddenly threw yourself onto me and begin crying and kissing my hands. (You have a way of doing this which is quite endearing but too threatening for me). It was one of the most touching things I remember about you.

I told your friends that I was standing by you. I didn't know if I was your therapist, lodger/housekeeper, or lover....

You invited me to Malta very early in our relationship. I was quite flattered, but I didn't really want to go. I believe that quality time is better spent at home.

I remember walking out on you three times during our relationship. Once was in Malta. I'd had enough of all the children's crying and their spoilt petulant behaviour.

I had been invited on holiday by a work colleague: a big Kenyan girl, who actually asked me through Pam. I got along with her very well, and she definitely liked me, but I went on holiday with you out of a sense of duty, and feeling I was a member of your family. I asked her what she thought of you after you had come to our barbecue. She said you were very pretty.

I remember that barbecue in the garden especially for one thing. You sat down on the grass with your legs up a little. I was really shocked to see very bad bruising all over your inner thighs high up. When I asked you about it you said that it had been caused by riding your old bicycle. The only other time I have seen bruises like that was with a girl I taught literacy skills to at the Trust. I saw them one day and wondered if I should report it because I suspected abuse at her home.
I met your aunty, and quite a few of your family. I was struggling to find anything to bond me to you though.

Do you remember going on the giant banana boat in Gozo harbour... and falling off?
Do you still have the pearl earrings I bought you on holiday?
I would have preferred to go abroad on our own rather than with Roger and his screwball entourage. It could have made a big difference. It might have helped.

One of the most enjoyable days I ever spent with you was playing at the side of the river in Wallingford, just beyond the bridge. We played for hours with a burst football, throwing it up in the air and catching it. We pretended to push Benji in the river and wouldn't let him get out of the water.
We were larking around there all afternoon.
Do you recall sitting on the high bench in the castle grounds? We often went there at the weekend.

I tried to understand you. I thought that one day my feelings might suddenly grow, but I struggled to find a way to connect to you. I even wondered if you had a soul. You seemed to be so disconnected somehow.
 I think it's a mistake to think that people have to be very alike to get along though. It may have been my intuition telling me something. From the moment I first drove up to you front door I kept telling myself; if this goes wrong you could end up in serious trouble or you could even die.
I never really committed myself fully to you. I am extremely sorry for being so disingenuous. You must have been very confused.
You once said to me; "You don't come here for sex, so what do you come here for.... I don't do a thing for you do I? I can feel it."

I didn't like drinking wine every night, although I often went out to that off-licence in town. They must have got sick of seeing me I went there so many times for you in the evening. Wine gives me a headache. I could quite happily go the rest of my life without a drink. My dad had a bad drink problem and I never wanted to be like him. I used to check your phone sometimes, and all it had on it were messages from me and Penny...You said you had fallen out with her, and then I would find you both drinking together in the garden.
I am sorry I used the 'thing' with you. How did I ever sink to that? Some people might see the funny side, but it should never be a substitute for normal loving. I saw you sat up in bed looking at it once. I don't think you really liked it, although

you said you knew someone who would. You stripped off on the sofa to use it once. I used to hide it under the stairs. Then it suddenly disappeared. You thought Rose might have found it. How embarrassing...

You pleaded to stay with me at Grays road one night. The laptop was on my bedside cabinet when we decided to watch a film. When I turned it on the most hard-core porn suddenly started playing.

It was a short clip of something which had turned up in my e-mail and I had started watching. I suppose we all get a bit bored sometimes, but I hated to think of you knowing I watched things like that. I remember you sitting up in the bath at Grays road, and me shampooing and washing your hair.

I got to the point where I didn't even want to scratch your back in bed. I used to turn over and sleep at the other side. Sleeping has been a big problem for me for years and I fidget like mad sometimes. I don't find it at all easy to sleep when someone else is there. I know you were sad and confused by this. I was very aware of you lying there with your eyelashes fluttering wondering what you should do. I know you wanted to sleep with your head on my chest but it felt too intense. You once called out 'help!' You once crept your hand slowly up my leg.

All you wanted was to be close to someone. I am very sorry I found that such a strain. I like privacy and solitude. I even went to sleep in the spare room sometimes as Brian had done.

You even found me on the floor in the spare shower-room once.

You started to drink more. I went to the house one evening quite late to find you in a terrible state in bed. I can't even describe how bad. I don't think it was at all good for the little ones.

You said: "you're never going to give up your job to be with me!"
You asked me about my bank account and how much I was worth.
I did offer to help you pay your mortgage. I did help where I could.

One evening you had fallen into a coma. I couldn't wake you and I got very worried. For ages I just sat and talked to you. I thought that maybe your soul would be listening to me somewhere. I found it very unsettling and I didn't really enjoy being with you. I wasn't comfortable.

That didn't stop me from trying to communicate with you and spreading little tears over your eyelids while you were slumbering. You told me that if I wanted sex I could touch you or do anything to you, even if you were asleep. If I could have found a way to find you more desirable I would have done. I have to apologise for touching you inappropriately while you were asleep. It wasn't nice, and it wasn't enjoyable. Ok, a little! While you were asleep on the sofa downstairs once I discovered you were wearing a pair of black knickers with a huge patch in the crutch which had been frayed to almost nothing.

You stopped smoking and then you had a fag in your mouth. I hate to see women smoking. Were you trying to tell me something? You had a hard look, which alarmed me...I don't know where it came from.

We went out for a meal with Adam at Waterstones.
It was in the middle of the Michael Jackson court case.

You went off to buy one of his CD's...

When I first met Benji he was on his own. I was shocked by how small and young
he was. He was only seven or eight. I remember what a sweet little voice he had.
I think he knew it as well. He would sit beside me when we played on the
computer or while watching telly. I couldn't understand how easily he kept beating me
at world cup soccer. I saw you watching us through the kitchen window as we
played at shooting-in on the lawn.
I wanted to teach him so many things. About empathy and trust. How to behave
and how to write.
I went off to buy him a new football down at the shop because he asked for one.
When I came back he just kicked it in the corner. I suddenly realized he had
several footballs there already.
I never saw kids with so many bluddy toys and things lying around. Their bedrooms
were full of them and they were always getting more.
His leg went a bit septic once, so I went out every day to the chemist to buy him
some antiseptic dressing and clean his wound. You wanted me to take him to
football practise which I did.
At night he would come and bang on the bedroom door or throw things if he
heard a sound. You said he had once walked in on you...
I didn't like the way there was no privacy, and there was a lodger, with people
coming and going all the time. The atmosphere seemed strange. Something
seemed to be missing...
Then I met Emily. A bright funny little girl with lots of character.
They reminded me of my sister and me. Both very different but also remarkably similar.
The only person who came between us was 'Catty.' It was a bluey-grey colour.
She called it Catty. It had whiskers. It could have been a mouse. She carried it
everywhere and would cry if it wasn't there.
Do you remember a little tin doll I gave her on her birthday? She burst into tears
when she saw it. It was nice. You laughed at her.
I once brought her some rock back from the seaside. She pranced up the stairs.

What a little show-off. She was definitely a little girl!

She still trailed around with her dummy in. She was a bit old for one, but it would have been cruel to take it off her. It suited her.

I often read her a bedtime story until she fell asleep. The last story I remember reading to them both was 'the Magician's Nephew' which was one of my old favourites. I'm sorry I never managed to finish it. Roald Dahl's Big Friendly Giant was another one. I read it to them more than once.

You told Penny we were finished, and then she saw us together at the pool.

I remember swinging Emily round in the garden by her ankles and throwing her up high into the air in the swimming pool at the Phoenicia in Valetta. She reminded me of myself in some ways and I will always miss them.

The children never seemed to have a proper breakfast. Everything was done at a pace without any real organisation.

I remember putting on her shoes halfway down the stairs one morning....

We were coming back from the fish shop in Wallingford one night. Her tiny little frame was sat in the passenger seat of my Mitsubishi Warrior. I thought it would make a good family car. I remember going to buy it with you.

She suddenly said; "Andrew. Who do you love most. Me or mummy?"

I thought for a while. We weren't getting along too well by this stage.

"I love you both the same but in different ways," I eventually said.

And I always will no matter where she is or how big she gets.

We went to a ballet concert, the first I had every been to, at the little theatre in Wallingford. You were acting bizarrely for some strange reason. If we had been really getting along I would have held your hand all through the performance. It was your behaviour which put me off you. For an intelligent woman you seemed to be so shallow and fickle.

Emily sat on my knee as usual. I wish I could have hugged her more, but she would probably have squirmed and tried to get away.

I leant forward and kissed her little head. You were there. Some of her hairs got stuck to my mouth. She always smelt nice.

She sometimes cheated at cards. I think you should have told her not to do that.

She once pretended to comb my hair....so she obviously had a great sense of humour.

She had a little pound money container. I didn't like you to encourage it, but I didn't have the heart to discourage it either. Reluctantly I made a donation.

After Emily realised Benji could get away with staying in our bed she thought she could too. In the end we all slept together in a heap. I think it's called 'pigging.' It bonded me a lot with you all, and it made me feel left out when I came in at night later and saw you all together.

If I had to leave I always kissed you all before I left. I was always happy for them to be there and I never wanted to push them away or take them anywhere else except their own home.

I don't think it did anything to help our love-life, but it did bring us close together. It gave me a break from the pressure of trying to satisfy you. Who knows. It might have happened naturally one day.

I admit that I have had my problems.
"Are you going to be my new daddy now?" asked Emily.

There isn't anything I wouldn't have done to protect and guard them both from harm. If Emily had been mine I don't think I could ever have left her, and I would have taken her round with me everywhere I went. When you first introduced us she was standing through the door in the lounge. I felt an immediate bond. She took my hand and dragged me around with her for weeks.
No matter how much I loved her, I could never have loved one more than the other. I will never forgive you for turning them both against me and robbing me of their most precious years. They must be so old now, it makes me want to cry.
You might think that what happened before we met was not important.
You might wonder why I have to mention these things now, but I do...!
I met a wonderful attractive lady with reddish brown hair called Mary Holmes (I knew her first us 'Lizzie'). She is the reason why they found the things they did. She was intelligent as well as very beautiful. Some people just have it.
When I went to meet her I always felt happy. A nightingale sung in my heart. When she nestled her head in my lap, just like she used to do with her dad, and I put my arms around her with my head on hers it felt lovely. It felt like *true love*. One word one message from her and my heart seemed to soar up to paradise.
I only went with her three times, and even then, I was getting my headaches. I drove halfway across the country to see her and all the time it felt natural.
Even if she was asleep she could hear me speaking and would answer me.
The trouble is: every man who met her seemed to feel the same way.
She was tall: nearly six foot.
She told me that I was a really nice guy, but that she needed someone to make her feel small. To be honest I do like tall women, but I hate having to stand on tip-toe. I was devastated and felt very ill. My face actually started to swell up.
She'd been married to a six-foot five black American basketball player. Her parents had begged her not to marry him, but she said he was unbeatable in bed. She said that marrying him was the worst mistake of her life, yet she said that it would not put her off going with another one. I decided that it was the final straw. I would do a couple more paintings and make one final collection of poems before ending it all. I still needed to find a way. Then I met you....

I came over to work in Oxford after being offered a really lucrative job with a reputable academic family close by. It also meant that my then girlfriend could visit me more easily. She lived near Coventry and was a Probation Officer. She was very pretty with blonde hair and big blue eyes. We were perfect in every way except one. She was very sociable and relaxed, while I am a hermit who likes to live in a cave.

I am very confident, but I'm also a great perfectionist.

We first met on the train to Oxford, and walked around hand in hand all day. She was a really lovely person, and there was certainly some good chemistry, but even with her I was a complete idiot sometimes and couldn't act normally. She put up with it for a long time though. I think she really cared for me and she didn't want to see me get hurt. After we went to Florence together I checked her e-mail and found out she had been with an ex-boyfriend just after we had a slight tiff. Unbeknown to me he had been pestering her for months.

I just knew something was wrong: apart from me I mean. We were about to take a bus trip around Florence and we climbed on board. She sat half-way down the bus. I walked all the way down to the back. She started crying....

I carried her little picture around in my pocket and slept with it under my pillow for over a year...

I was five years old when I first saw Lydia. She had just started school. I remember her being brought into our classroom and blushing near the door just as I had done. I loved her all the way through school.

When I was eleven my mum and dad were going through a very unhappy divorce. My dad used to get very violent when he had been drinking, and a lot of it was directed against me.

We were in the top class, and due to leave. We were due to go to different schools. I remember agonising for months how to tell her how I felt but never did even though I saw her looking at me sometimes. *I found it easy to tell my mum.*

I was sixteen when I saw her walking with her sister down the street. She lived on the next street to my uncle and grandmother. Everyone could see that she was pregnant. I knew from that day that I could never ever be happy. When I was about forty-three someone sent me some details from a dating agency. I rang the owner and managed to get her phone number. The woman who answered could have been my Lydia. She talked about her family having to flee Eastern Europe at the beginning of the last war. I wrote a long letter to her, and only at the end did I tell her about the girl I used to know. I was working down in Kent at the time.

She rang my mum wanting to speak to me. She wrote a very sincere and heartrending letter all about her life.

She spoke about a toy soldier I had given to her in the school playground when I was eight. It had been very important to me but I had forgotten all about it. She also brought back other memories I had forgotten (and I thought I had a good memory). She spoke about a little boy at school who was like her in every way.

She said: "Andrew, we all have problems, just different ones!"

"The soul is immortal, and lives far beyond this space and time."

She said: "this is the love I would have always wanted..."

I found her very deep and moody though. She warned me about how hurtful she could be...Lydia was still living with someone in a large house on the outskirts, but they were getting divorced she told me.

She would ring me in the middle of the night and beg me to take her away.

I had her in bed several times but I just couldn't find any desire.

When I couldn't or wouldn't make love to her she burnt all my letters and sent them back to me in the post...

When I opened her package, I could feel my heart stop beating. I nearly fainted.

That's the first time I ever thought about ending my own life.

You once said that you had done when Brian left.

As you know, I once worked for *the Samaritans*.

I managed to persuade a gangster in Chicago to send me a revolver disguised as automobile parts. I told him it wasn't to hurt anyone else, but that I knew someone who wanted to end their own life. It was nothing to do with me hurting anyone else: it was about being a failure and worrying about growing old. Too many things had gone wrong to mention. I was close to someone in my early twenties, but lost her. He said he would send me a handful of bullets to practise with. I had no idea what dum-dum bullets were or how to fire a gun. I wasn't even sure what a firing pin was. He said that he didn't know if it would be any good to me...

I tried to contact him again because it kept falling apart and seemed to be welded in the middle but his phone didn't answer.

It had a swastika on the barrel, and appeared to be from the First World War, a Browning revolver, with 'museum de Belgique' stencilled on it....

I was scared to go near it and kept moving it from place to place.

I told myself that I would not change my mind.

That was when I met you. The gun was nothing to do with you. It was just a silly idea: although we all have to die some day, and I would rather it was quick. My stepfather was dying of cancer and is still suffering today (Keith died in 20120).

I should have thrown it away or just talked to someone about how I was feeling.

You knew something was wrong but I didn't think you would be able to cope with what I told you. Quite understandably you would have been very worried about me. I bottled it all up every night and that is why I behaved like I did.

That is why, even when you were doing your best to love me, even when you were following me around all weekend so I didn't abuse myself and flooding me with affection, I couldn't open up and say anything.

I must say I have always been a bit of clown. I have played a number of practical jokes over the years, but nothing as bad or as serious as the ones which followed.

Benji had gone to his friends in Eyam when I decided to close the place I had been renting in Wymondham. It was costing me a fortune, and I was hardly ever there. We went across to pick up all my things with Emily.

You made me call at my mums, but they were out. I wonder if that would have changed anything, if you had met. Keith had to go to hospital.

I really regretted Benji not being there. My mum would have loved him. She would have really spoiled him. I greatly regret him missing her, because I think he would have loved it too. My mum has a great way with children, EXCEPT HER OWN.

I remember getting some fresh prawns and going down to the beach in Sheringham. You were really annoying me and I was ready to finish with you when we got back. I suppose I must have appeared very grumpy and bad tempered. I couldn't sleep and I felt unhappy and under a lot of pressure.

Emily changed on the beach and went to splash in the sea. She was very funny and loved every minute of it. I went in as well.

I got some paint things out at the house to give her something to do. I still have a painting she did.

I am really sorry I couldn't be more normal with you. I am really sorry I worried you. I was horrible to you, and you didn't really deserve it. You were still very loving. Your attitude was strange. I didn't feel any connection with you and your ways. You once said that you were even more sensitive than me.

I drove back as quickly as I could without uttering a word. When we got near home you said; "Can't you drive any faster?"

I told you that you should be more loyal to people. I am sorry I ignored you for most of the journey or remained silent.

When I returned to Grays road you sent me a message to say you didn't want to see me any more. I couldn't have blamed you, but after all the attention you'd given me, if anyone was going to finish with anyone it was going to be me!

I went round to Rose and Dennis's. I couldn't believe it when he told me to go away or he would call the police. I thought he was being a very horrid little man.

When I eventually found you we made up and I stayed the night again.

I might have been a lot closer to you than I thought.

I helped you with repairs and did all sorts of chores which needed doing around the house. You said that Brian had never bothered.

Property

When we returned from Norfolk I put some of my possessions into the garage, and some in the house. These included:

☐ A brand new large screen TV
☐ Some of my favourite DVD's
☐ A brand new hi-fi (which resided under the fish tank)
☐ A new DVD recorder
☐ A brand new mountain bike for you to use in place of your old one (we went out sometimes at the weekend in an effort to get you fitter or did some running on the hill)
☐ A new web-cam
☐ I left some of my best CD's in your stack and I bought you some new ones

I did a small watercolour which you hung above the fish tank...behind it I stuck a note :- 'you gave me a dream of a happy home and family, something I never really had, and I gave you this little picture, which I mistakenly thought would be my last'

I left a large picture of you in the garage. I think I had your face brilliant at one point, but I took it a bit too far as usual...

I left you a selection of books...

In one of the books I wrote - 'for Benji and Emily - I love you both....'

Car boot sales

We did a few car boot sales together, mainly at the Kassam.

Do you remember me in the back of the pick-up giving away almost everything I owned for next to nothing? Bottles of wine, mini TVs - everything. I sold a lot of other things when you weren't there. You went off to get some drinks and a bacon sandwich with the kids. I think some items were stolen because I couldn't keep my eyes on everyone.

You looked puzzled and a little confused.

You kept wondering why I was giving away all my worldly goods: well now you know...! You told the fuzz I had sold everything I had at the sales.

You even betrayed me with your neighbours.

That dog of theirs was like Sherlock bloody Holmes; always picking up my scent.

Internet dating

I had relationships with a lot of different women from all around the world while living in Oxford. I saw the way people went from one partner to another. I never wanted you to behave the same. It seemed such a waste of time and effort.. I think the best relationships develop and deepen over time. And, you deserved better.

You told me you had met two other people between Brian and me.

One was a vicar with funny shoes, and the other one worked in a supermarket at Didcot (I found a message from him saying he had to go home but that he didn't want to). You told me you didn't want to see him but he kept pestering you?

Just before you I met Honor. She mixed with some of the Royal family and her relatives owned land all over the place, with a restaurant in Italy. I'd seen 'it' all before we met. She was very into exhibitionism, which I really wasn't.

She brought a lot of presents when she came over including some wine and some cheeses. She gave me a little handmade bible which she had been given in Mexico. She had written 'I love you' inside.

Honor was very bright and sensual, but we were like chalk and cheese

When I came home one day you told me you had been with three different men that week while I was away.

You told me that you wished the sexual side had worked better in our relationship because it would have brought us a lot closer together.

When I checked your phone and e-mail it appeared to be true.

One of the messages said; 'right thing wrong time, I enjoyed it too!'

You said that you had only just met one of them on the street. I was under a lot of pressure at the time. I would like to tell you why. I still didn't want to touch you. You told me that you wouldn't be bothered if you went with five different men from the Internet in a week. Before it had been only me.

You told me one of them was only interested in sex.

You said that you wouldn't mind using the internet for sex.

I told you I didn't want to lose you.

I didn't know what to say or what to believe.

You said I already had.

I saw your eyes water when you looked at me.

You said you were going to marry someone called Dave.

You said you could feel it.

I said, "but you haven't even met him yet...!"

It was all very confusing. I didn't know what to do.

Then you told me that you thought you might have dreamt it all...

I had wondered about some kind of threesome to get me interested. I once left Rachel a note near the washing machine one night. She sometimes came down to unlock the door for me. It was very brazen.

You were snoring away upstairs. I asked her if she wouldn't mind coming and sucking on your breasts for half an hour....

I couldn't believe it when she thought for a while, and then said ..." Oh, alright!"

I didn't take her up on it and left soon after, but your voice sounded a bit quaky when I spoke to you on the phone the next day.

I came back one night and you told me to go away or you would call the police.

I had a key cut when you left me to go off to work.

When I went back the next night you asked me if I would be staying all week.

You were in a terrible state. I had a pretty good idea you had been with someone. I still felt nothing except confusion: no real feelings. I told you that you didn't have to behave like that.

You were lying in Emily's bed when we started petting.

You told me David had brought an overnight bag the first time you met. You went to pick him up at Cholsey station. I've hated the place ever since.

The men you went with all seemed to fizzle out. You told me that you might have sex with me next, or it could be someone else.

I thought your behaviour just wasn't right.

Your tongue was wagging about as I looked down on you in the light from the doorway.

"If you could make love with anyone in the whole world who would it be?" I asked.

You hesitated a second and said...

"You?!"

What can I say?

Your craziness was exasperating. Perhaps I had started to care about you. It's the one thing I do miss a bit.

The love I had only felt in your hands started to come back again. Perhaps you are a Healer like me...?

I woke up one night with you feeling the top of my head. You shot back. Bound to be curious I guess. I wasn't angry. It was quite sweet.

Then one night your arm suddenly flopped over me.

You laughed when I made a funny sound in bed.

We started having sex during one of your periods and I got your blood all over me...another time I found you wearing knickers in bed.

You asked me if I would be taking my things when I went.

66

I left them because I always thought I would come back...
And I never wanted you to forget me.

AN INCIDENT

In August something really bad happened. You kept asking me what was wrong.
You said there was something wrong. *You told me about a dream you had. You
had gone somewhere to see me. Some of your friends were there. The flatfoots
were there too, but they wouldn't let you into the building to see me.* It was a stupid petty
little business, which was blown right-out-of-proportion. I was struggling to know
what to do with you. I was bored and fed-up. My life just didn't feel at all happy,
and I wasn't cut out for balloon dancing.
I didn't do anything sexual. I suppose I just like to shock people sometimes. I really
should know better. It was a very silly thing to happen. All it brought me was
misery. I told you that I'd had an argument with someone in town. I was very
ashamed of letting you down.
I called in a shop on the High street and started trying on clothes. One of the
assistants came back with a pair of trousers and when she handed them over
through the changing room curtain she saw that I was only half dressed, and that
was all. She turned and walked away without reacting. One or two seconds at
most. The Assistants could be seen acting out what had happened on the shop video. I
walked calmly out of the door. The street was quite empty.
No matter what you think about these things, it certainly doesn't deserve the title
'Sex-offender,' and I did not deserve the awful repercussions which followed.
It wasn't something I could really talk to you about even though you ran a clinic
on sexual health. I was still taking the pills you got me for a healthy willy though.
The Authorities must have known about me and you. I am surprised they didn't
come rushing around to tell you bad things about me even then...?
Shortly after it happened you were leaving work and the miserable toads fined
you for not wearing your seat belt.

About three weeks after the original incident I cycled into town down Headington
hill and saw there were people in plain clothes *and* uniforms all around.
When I came out of Boots the chemist four officers jumped me and dragged me in
handcuffs through the crowded streets to the main police station. I decided to
plead guilty to exposure and wrote the manager of the shop a letter of apology. I
just couldn't face a lengthy court case.
I was held for ten hours while they played their pathetic games.
Poor Adam was at home wandering what had happened to me.
I spoke to Pam on the phone about what had happened. She was very
understanding. I sent her a text saying that no-one loved me.
She said that lots of people did.
Pam said I ought to tell you myself what had happened rather than you hear it
from someone else. We weren't getting along too well. Even if it had been
months before I would have found it hard to tell you.
You had just started your course at the college.
I needn't remind you that it was my idea that you did Osteopathy. You weren't

happy in your job. I suggested it because I had a friend called Clare Farleigh who had gone on to do it after nursing too.

I came up to see you. You were parked outside. You drove off.

You said that love had to come from both sides. What a bluddy cheek!

You'd started asking me if we were better just being friends. I recall going up the hill to the garden centre. What a cold mood you were in. I was really fed up with you.

I was there one night when you said you were expecting an important phone call or two. You had been away all weekend and your phone was switched off.

When I turned up and asked you where you had been you asked me what I was doing there. You flinched when I touched you. The first time I felt a twinge of desire you pushed me away.

You said you had stayed one night with Karen, and one night with your brother's friend. His wife didn't really like you staying. He was black I think. You said he had been suspended from his job in the Health service for a suspected sexual assault. You said he once made a pass at you.

You told me your breasts were sore because I had sucked them too hard.

When the phone rang you closed the door.

I sat on the sofa in the lounge and tried to hear what you were saying. It all sounded very deep and emotional. Your voice went quite high some of the time.

You said to whoever it was: "We are friends, aren't we?...you are the best friend I have ever had."

"Friends, yes! Yes I know you are having trouble with you wife..."

You looked quite secretive and cold when you returned.

Pam once asked me why I always seemed to meet such needy and perplexing women.

For weeks I had deliberately stayed away or went off somewhere else. I am a strange man sometimes I know. I had a special cake baked for your birthday, and I made you a card with a poem I'd written inside.

I also ordered you a large bouquet of flowers in Wallingford.

I went out to Woodstock shopping for you and found a brown fur jacket top. I bought you a size too small.

She said I could bring it back if you wanted to try a bigger one.

These I presented to you on your birthday.

I just turned up at the house like before.

You said that Penny had invited you out but that you would rather stop in with me.

You wore your new top, even though it was a bit of a squash. I am so sorry for that. I never got chance to change it for the right size.

I never got to taste any of that lovely cake either...

On Sunday you invited me to help you at Emily's birthday party.

Dennis was surprised to see me at the hall. We made friends. He'd had a lot of trouble with his eyes I think...

I helped to pay for the venue as you didn't have enough money.

It was a nice day and I remember us taking pictures of Emily running across the hall.

She was in her element.

I felt very tense. You pushed me away when I touched you which wasn't very nice and you made fun of me.

Rose noticed how you were treating me.

The clown said he thought I was with 'Rose.' Not very complimentary, but you did say Brian had a nice face.

That night I read Benji his story in bed as usual, but I had a splitting headache.

You asked me if I would be staying, but I had to get away to bed.

In the morning I appeared in Court all by myself.

I did my best, but still received a hefty fine.

What was even worse: they put me on the Sex offender's register for five years. It meant that the police would be calling round and interfering in my life. I also had the Probation department ringing my employers and trying to cause trouble.

I had just got back from Court when I received a text message from you. I could have done with all the help I could. I have never been sure to this day whether the police came to see you and tried to say the most nasty and unpleasant things about me.

Your text message said: 'I don't want to see you again. No further contact.'

My care of Adam was affected by what was going on and I greatly regret that.

I think that if he had ever seen you he would have run you down in his wheel chair.

Adam never knew about the Court case. He would have been too upset.

I still came round as you know. I didn't know what to say to you.

I sent you a text message. I was used to you being there.

You replied with the only truly hurtful message I have ever received from you; 'I don't know you!'

That is so true really. I never let you get to know me because I was never sure about you or the future.

I felt guilty that you had known me for eight months, during which time we had slept together on and off, and I had never let you into my heart or confided in you about anything which really mattered or which had altered my life...

I cycled all the way from Oxford just to look in the drive. I even saw Benji and Emily taking Fluffy out for a walk one morning, but I couldn't go near you..

On one occasion Benji came running from his friends to talk to me. He thought I was coming in, but I told him to go back.

Another time he actually blushed.

There was an occasion a few months later when you had a college teacher with you all morning: a Friday I think. He ran inside the house.

Benji: "I've just seen Andrew!"

You: silence.... then "Where was he?"

Benji: "Just outside..."

After your friend had gone...

You: "Did you really see Andrew? What did he do?"

Benji: "He just went away!"

You: "Don't talk to him!"

Benji: "Why not?"

"Why do you think...!?" you snapped.

You might wonder how I know all this...?

I looked at you one day, and decided you would be the wrong person to joke with.

You *said* I would see a different side to you.

You were in the kitchen with Sandra.

Let me tell you something about Sandra. I don't think she's had it as easy as you might think. You were always sensitive about her. Yes, I saw she was beautiful, but there is no way I could ever have touched her instead of you.

I sent you a message about wizards. It was only meant as a bit of light-hearted banter.

You replied (with Sandra): 'go and see a doctor. You are sick!'

And 'fuk off you impotent loser!'

If you thought things like that would hurt me you are very much mistaken, but you obviously thought they would hit me where it hurt. I thought they were very childish and petty comments to make, and they say a lot more about the kind of person you are than me.

I was shocked that you could send messages like that though.

By the way. I never sent you twenty messages a day. You were lucky if you got one or two. I often ignored your messages and never even replied to them!

I once rode past you on the field. You were standing with your arms round Emily...

<u>The reasons I came back and what I did there</u>:

I came back because, strange to say it, I actually missed you, and it felt like home...

I had often left in the middle of the night to get some sleep.

I had often turned up late because that was the only time I could get away and because I liked to read their bedtime story and tuck you all in.

One day you stopped right next to me in the car at the traffic lights. Emily stared at me through the window and seemed very puzzled. I was staying in the George hotel down the road at great expense.

You were on the computer with them one night. You talked to them about the *devil's number.* You had obviously discussed it with them before.

I wonder what they will think of you when they get older?

I sent you a message about once a month, but each time I did I was there watching you in the garden.

Maybe I just like spying on people. I do like finding out about people's little secrets. It was a teeny bit creepy!

I wanted to see your reaction and I actually learnt a lot more about you during this time.

You once tracked your ex all the way to Spain (the German guy who you met as his nurse in hospital) and groped his partner. You said there was nothing there (she was "as flat as a pancake!"). So, you know all about this kind of behaviour?

You once questioned me: "You wouldn't ever hurt me if we fell out, would you?" What a silly thing to ask! It was almost as daft as asking me if I would touch Benji or Emily. Not in a million bluddy years! I thought it was stupid and insulting.

I saw you in the restaurant we used to go to, with Mat R.

He didn't take his glasses off even when you massaged his back.

You kept referring to me as 'the nutter.' Thanks!

I saw you take out the photograph album when he had massaged your chest.

You touched his leg.

I watched for a few moments. It was so boring. I felt a bit sorry for both of you and went home.

You left his address at the side of the sofa. He used you just for the night and you had probably done likewise.

I spoke to him disguised as another woman on-line.

He bragged about fking you listening to the BG's on my hifi.

I woke about ten the next morning with a horrible impression. I could feel and hear what you were doing. It was truly awful. I could hear you crying 'ouch...' he bragged about a...l intercourse. What on earth were you doing letting a creep like him do that to you!? I could hear a lot of panting and grunting.

He didn't come back. He must have been quite sane after all.

The next time I saw you after Christmas you looked awful...your hair was very bedraggled and you looked pale and drawn. You looked very upset and unwell. I t may have been me. You reported me for leaving some poetry in a drawer, and a Christmas card on the wall.

I was out in the garden when I sent you one of my rare messages. I was watching you carefully, but I couldn't go across or do anything. The paper with his address and phone number was still at the side of the couch.

I texted you: 'I miss u' - that was all.

I saw you read it and nod your head. You started weeping and touched your face. I am so sorry for any pain I have caused you....

I left you a bottle of wine sometimes and other things as well. I wrote a note on the back of my kitchen board until you took it down.

It was the one with a duck on the front, which had hung on my kitchen wall for years.

I thought it was especially funny to write notes in your Calendar, like 'apologise to Andrew'... (in December).

I am a very sentimental person really. I thought that one day you would understand me better.

A WPC I met at a party in Southampton advised me not to have anything more to do with you. She warned me you were trouble and to keep away from you. She said you were the one with the problem.

I remember Howard insisting: "She's reported you once. She'll do it again!"

He was furious about my antics. You had once sat down in 'his' chair.

I deliberately set you up with a black guy called Massi to see how you would react. It was a silly thing to do. I gave him your name on 'lovenfriends.'

He was nasty piece of work. He went around seducing white women on line and then he would display the pictures he took, so everyone could see.

I used to read your e-mails between each other. He contacted you under two different names. In one he pretended to be white.

The last thing I knew about him he was living in Croydon.

I once rang him to find out about you but he was very slippery. Not even my Private detective friend in Yorkshire could get him to give away any information. His usual voice-mail message said: "life is a box of chocolates. You never know what you are going to find...."

I put a photo of you up on line a few months later. He obviously recognised you, and seemed to know a lot about you. He said he wanted to meet someone who was passionate, very sexual, and could keep a secret. He also said he was into Dildos and oral sex. He told me that he had never visited Oxford.

You told him that I had put a picture which looked like you on-line...

{A man listed as living at your address but also with a business address in Oxford called Calvin Shields sold marital aids and sex aids on the Internet).

You told a policewoman who called at my place of work that I had put your details on line, because someone told you.

One evening before you met 'Kevin,' you dressed yourself in black with little ringlets in your hair I had never seen before, and were gone all night.

You looked a bit the worse for wear the next day, but not as bad as before. Your hair looked a bit matted.

In 2006 you sent me a sexually explicit voice-mail message when you thought it was Massi who had texted you. You said that you had once had an incredible sexual experience in your car and that you hoped he would respond. I think you were a bit drunk to be honest. There's a turn up *for the book!*

I am sorry for playing these silly games with you. It would take a lot of explaining...

I was very unhappy when I saw you meeting regularly with Kevin Br. Naturally I read all your messages. It lasted a lot longer than I thought it would. I saw Roger in Wallingford. He told me that he was alright but that he wasn't used to dealing with children. I was there the first night you introduced him to the kids. You kept going back to see how they were getting on.

I heard you telling someone on the phone that all Kevin did was stuff himself with cream cakes all day and talk about his ex-wife.

You told them that he certainly wasn't the one for you.

You actually described him as 'sweet!'

I went in once when he had hurt his foot and couldn't visit you that weekend. He preferred to go out with 'the boys' anyway, he said.

You were in a poorly state in the small room at the front. You had made it into a little bedroom. I felt really sorry for you, and went close to you a few times but was frightened to wake you up because I wasn't sure how you would react. You seemed so lonely and alone.

I hated you making fun of me with the kids and their friends.

I hated you playing games at the window and kissing him when you thought I was outside.

I hated seeing his car there, seeing him pawing at your chest, attempting to kiss you, wiping his saliva away, lying on his chest, slopping wine.
I wanted it to end....I thought that I would forgive you though.

I found Massimo's details on your phone when I came in one night.
You saw me once in the garden, I think, I don't know how. You went on the phone. I was questioned by a police car which suddenly appeared from nowhere on the High street.
I went back and saw you were absolutely paralytic.
You were on the sofa all alone and looking very unhappy.
I looked at you and said out loud from the garden: "I love you!"
It was as if you could hear me.
The reaction from you was very upsetting.
You burst into tears like I had never seen before. They were rolling in big lumps down your cheeks and you were sobbing. You started nodding your head exactly as I said it. Could it be that we were linked in some mysterious way?
You got up after a while but you were very rocky and fell, breaking a glass.
Fluffy was petrified. He hissed and ran into the corner of the room.
As you lay on the floor he was meowing loudly in consternation.
I let myself in and cleaned up the glass, then I lifted you up onto the sofa and covered you with a blanket, and then left. I think Kevin had gone to bed to sleep off the booze.
I was there the first night that Yas stayed. I thought he looked Chinese.
He kept dusting the side of the sofa. You were upstairs, and when you came down you had a lot of eye makeup on. You kept licking your lips. He had gone upstairs by then. He seemed a pleasant enough fellow. He told you that relationships were never equal. He said Kevin looked like a *used car salesman*. Yas was always looking for more from you. Originally you told him: "friends, just friends, yes?!"
Yas started coming across on a Friday at a time when Kevin wasn't coming as often. I heard you in the garden begging Kevin not to go, just as you had done with me.
He came round for the last time at Christmas. You kissed him at the doorstep.
I came back to see Fluffy, sit him on my lap, talk to him, feed him, and clean his tray, which was really disgusting sometimes.
I mended your door which was sticking.
I checked *my property* and your phone. You left your mobile out in the garden more than once.
I put the boot down on your car because you had left it open all night and it was blowing in the wind.
I took some milk to make a drink.
I used to come in late at night and look at you in bed with Benji and Emily holding you on either side. I turned the light off once and you woke up. You must have known it was me. You told Anna: "It's my Stalker. He comes in at night, but I don't think he's dangerous." She was on the Osteopathy course with you.
I left some chocolates in your coat pockets (which I believe you handed

73

round to friends) – the Cops came to interview me about them as you know because Debbie G. showed you my book. Didn't you ever see the advert...Cadbury's milk-tray? I didn't even know it was a crime.

I was in and out like a jack-in-a-box one night. You were lying in bed. The kids should have been there, but I couldn't see them anywhere. You were all alone I think. It was now or never. God, did the floor in your bedroom creak. Back and forth like a yo-yo. Eventually I leaned over and kissed you ever so lightly on your forehead. You stirred and moaned a little. I was scared what you might do if you saw me. It was the first time I had touched you in months. It was very tender. I turned and walked carefully away...

On your 43rd birthday you must have been out somewhere. You were dozing on the downstairs sofa. Your face looked a little thinner. I wondered what it had been through since we were friends. I didn't touch you. I just stood there looking. Your dress was rucked up and your nylons all hanging down. I felt quite sorry for you. I took some flower petals from my pocket and scattered them in your lap. I didn't dare leave any obvious evidence of my visit because I didn't want any more pigs embarrassing me at work.

I left you another bottle of wine.

I took a pair of your used knickers (to my surprise they were very intoxicating).

I left two little jugs. You kept some papers in one. I heard you say to Rose; "I don't know where they came from!"

I made them myself in Adam's Barn kiln nearby....

I played tricks on you with the keys. I sometimes took them from your keyring and had them for all the doors. I thought I had lost the front door key once so went in and took the only one you had. I am extremely sorry for that. I heard you outside trying to get in. You had to go around to Rose's. I heard Benji and Emily sighing; "locked out of our own home!"

I left a little bonnet I had bought at the British library for Emily. I hope she wore it.

I left your Christmas presents under the tree.

I checked my note to see if it was still there, and when it wasn't replaced it with a carbon copy (as you know!).

I wrote in your address book.

I signed you up to an internet telephone account and monitored your calls.

I twiddled with my thumbs and wondered what to do next.

I used the loo, or had a bath.

I read all your post.

I changed some of the labels on your Osteopathy skeleton.

I went to the garage.

I moved your vase. The one you had tried to hide behind when Yas was there.

I turned your bedroom light on and off.

I went through your drawers and checked your wardrobe.

I left a photo in one of my psychology books.

I asked myself various questions, like;

Do you think this is bordering on obsession?

What if she finds out...

What is going to happen?

How do you think this is all going to end?

I just didn't want you to forget me! As if you ever could.

I kept a large notebook of my activities. It was really just a wind-up. I kept it out of boredom. I needed something to occupy my mind.

I have always liked mystery and suspenders.

A chap called Shane rang you. He arranged to meet you while you were out at Dennis's. He was from Mauritius. He told me you were keen on his nationality but you weren't sure about him being follically challenged and over fifty. If I remember rightly you said that anyone who wasn't married and hadn't had kids by the age of fifty wasn't fit for anything. You left his details in the cat basket. Then you met Danny. He was the one with 'piggy-eyes.' You told him about me, and went to the pub up the hill. The one we used to go to on a Sunday. You both looked at the sidewall when you drove in the cul-de-sac. He started groping your chest on the sofa. Not again I thought.

By that time Yas had gone up to bed. You left him in the house by himself. He appeared content to step aside but you could tell what he was thinking and where he wanted it to lead.

You were dressed in your usual red cardigan when you went out with Danny that night, and you had applied a lot of make-up. When you came back your face was very pale and you looked terrible. All your make-up seemed to be gone. When Danny started groping you seemed very nervous, but still flung your head in his lap. It all seemed so unreal. As if you were just acting a part.

Yas went to the upstairs window and looked out into the garden. I thought he might have seen me dashing across.

You were quiet the next night and sat with your back to the window. You looked a bit self-conscious talking to Yas and Anna.

Yas liked it better when it was just you and him. He joked about having to lock his door at night, and paying you in sex instead of board.

You 'glared' for a long time...

"Friends, just friends!" you said. You took it in turns to go on-line. You told Jo you had spent the last four days together. It was pouring down outside.

You read Yas Kevin's e-mail when he finished with you. Kevin said he had wanted to finish with you before but he couldn't because Alex (your new lodger) was there.

I sent you a message about having your back scratched.

Yas told you that you if you scratched someone's back they would have to do the same for you.

I recall him pretending to expose to you, and playing games at the bathroom window.

You told him about the church in London and your friends there.

You bragged to him about being a 'Scorpio.'

That night you sat there applying heavy lipstick and doing your nails. You kept applying lip-gloss, as he sat behind you.... I couldn't see if he was touching your bra-strap or not.... your eyelids began flickering nervously, then you looked very worried and self conscious, then you looked very hard and a bit upset, and got up. You went back to the computer. He castigated himself, as if he had missed his chance. You both kept on going to the bathroom.

The next message I sent you was a bit of tease.

I said that you were bound to turn someone on if you had your white breasts and pink nipples sucked.

You told Yas I was your Stalker, and that you couldn't stand me. I heard you saying the same thing about him on the phone.

You sent me a message with him at your side and asked for his help. It said; 'squishy little pink dick' and (once more) the well-worn 'fuk off u impotent loser!' He was quite submissive most of the time.

I went in one night and heard you open your door and pretend to scream to see if he would come to your room.

Sandra the Vicar's wife asked you if he *smelled*.

When you showed him a picture of Danny. Not a very attractive person by all accounts, Yas said, "well maybe he has a big dick?"

You replied: "I don't like it when you talk like that!"

All this seems so familiar...

You asked him if he found you 'boring.'

You sat there on the couch, almost laughing, playing with your bra-strap, sneaking a look at his face. You even had Anna in on the act one night, while I was freezing out in the garden in the pouring rain....

I left a poem about Fluffy for Benji. You took it down after a few weeks. Apparently, Emily found it and wouldn't go in the Wendy house again.

I don't know why, but Yas seemed to have decided to keep himself to himself. You asked him if he would like to go on holiday to Malta: "I'm on my own and so are you. The kids would love it!"

He asked you to ask him again in the middle of the week when you were *more sober*.

You wondered if he would like to start a business in Malta...

He said it didn't matter if you were 42-3 and he was 27?

You told him that you couldn't give him any children though...

He suddenly jumped up from our purple sofa and went to bed.

You sat there for ages by yourself, licking your lips and fantasizing. Putting your hair up, and letting it down again. Then you fell over spilling your glass.

I don't know what happened when you eventually went up to bed, but I got bored of sitting around and trying to stand in that little infant chair to see more.

The next night your face was very flushed as you rushed around his bedroom changing the bed sheets...

The next weekend Yas was there with Anna. Benji was on the Osteo couch. He was stroking his head and talking to him the way I used to do.

You were a little the worse for wear, but went in the kitchen and started talking to Anna. You told her that he was 'very sexual' and that you had had sex.

The next night you were by yourself at your computer touching yourself.
A strange thing happened while I was at my caravan round the corner doing your
portrait. I put your picture next to a decent picture of me to see what we looked
like together. It was very sad to see: we might have been a lot closer than I
imagined. I couldn't wait any longer:
I sent what I believed to be my final book of poetry to your father (and I thought
you were mad! _And_ you said _he_ was mad!).
As a Professor of Literature, I thought he would preserve my work and when I was
dead appreciate my sincerity. You told me your dad had once lain down in front
of the car to prevent you all from going to church one Sunday morning. You said he
lived with a gay man at Oxford, but still managed to get a Double First.
You were down in Wales with Sandra going through my book the next weekend...
When you came back you took my picture down again because of something I
had written inside my book and left the picture on top of the table...I wasn't going to
put a message behind it a third time if that's what you were thinking!
I once spoke to your father about Shakespeare. He was drinking a cup of tea after
breakfast on the living-room sofa. He wanted to know how I could quote from every
tragedy. When your parents visited I acted normally and tried to get on with them both.
Even though you said your mother was a 'bitch' I was determined to give them a
chance and treated them both with respect.
I can get along well with anyone who likes words and literature.
I thought you took after him quite a bit in other ways.
I never noticed your mum's legs. She is quite old. I found her to be more sensitive
than you made out.
 Your father kept ruffling his head and looking at me. Never seen a bald one before....
I never made a proper effort to dress up smartly and conduct myself in the way I
know I can. It was because I had given up on life.
 I used to leave my shoes and clothes at the side of the bed, and they were always
still there the next time I came.
We had a meal with your mum and dad at the table. Sandra was there too.
I was interested to discuss religion and politics with them. Your mum appeared to be a
very traditional Catholic and a monarchist.
I even stood up for your mum a bit when you began putting her down. That is why
I was a bit disappointed when you told me she said I "wasn't presentable" - a
doctor or a barrister like your brothers.
I didn't sell myself or make myself more acceptable. That was my frame of mind at
the time. I am very sorry for my failings.
She said they had only put up with your ex-husband for _your_ sake.

Pam once said of you that I 'could do a lot worse....'
When you came back from visiting your mum and dad the police tried to talk to
me but I ignored them. I could feel your mother's thoughts. She was very upset.
She must have read some of my book- '_small bird's sing_.' It needed additional editing.
I think she felt a bit sad about what was happening.
Adam suddenly died. You remember stopping at his house and meeting his

family...? He had suffered a huge aneurism in his head.

I was at his bedside holding his big toe when he slipped away. I had brought down all his cuddly toys to put round him at the John Radcliffe: his brown bear, his giraffe, and his blue sea-lion.

I sent you a message from his bedside. His sister was in tears.

You replied: 'fuk off, or u r nicked!'

You were lying on the sofa by yourself. I think you knew I would be round. I just wanted to put my arms round you and make everything alright, but I just couldn't do it. I was scared of someone coming down. The light was on in the bedroom even though it was very late. I went in and out several times, before I suddenly saw Benji at the top of the stairs looking down. He came down a step or two. I would have loved to reassure him, but I simply shut the door and went away. I went back to see him trying desperately to wake you up. His face was pouring with tears, poor lad. What did I ever do to make this happen. What did I ever do to make this poor little boy who I had carried in my arms to bed each night so afraid? I knew it was bound to happen one day after several close escapes.

You even came down one night in your blue nightie and missed me by a whisker. One time you sat with your head on the kitchen table. I couldn't have done this to anyone else. I think you'd passed out due to heat exhaustion.

It was you! Telling them stories. My behaviour was very silly, but I certainly didn't mean any harm. I wouldn't have hurt him for the world or harmed a single hair on his head. I wouldn't have hurt any of you in a million years, but I have been labelled along with the very worse type of people despite my saying this over and over again.

If only we had been able to talk instead of you sending silly messages and shaking your head. You were sitting there one night all alone and crying. You were wearing a pullover I had given you which my mum had knitted. I sent you a tease - "that's my mother's woolly pullover you're wearing...!" You nodded emotionally.

It was very touching seeing you in it and it made me cry.

You told Penny about my message...
She replied: 'scary-call the police!'
You told me Penny could be very two-faced.
The next night you locked the front door.
The night after that you didn't.

Crime and Punishment

I had just been to Adam's funeral. There were some lovely people there. It was all very moving. We were standing there in the quaint sunlit graveyard all together. I'd had my caravan on the site just round the corner for about a year.
Apparently, I *had* been spotted on the road.

I saw you in the supermarket. Tried not to look. You went back to be with Yas...you told the pigs I had parked my blue Landrover next to yours and reported me again. You nearly ran me down on my bike turning in ahead of me the short way to your work. I volunteered to be a 'guinea-pig' at the centre while you were training in the next room. I asked your colleagues not to tell you.... I saw you cycling across the bridge on the old bike on the other side.

I went in to see the Vicar of St Peter's to have a chat about us...

The church said I could go in any time.

You reported me for sitting with my bike on the bend.

I am sorry the children were upset and didn't understand.

Eventually I received a 'caution'.

I hated you behaving like a perfect stranger and telling everyone our relationship was never intimate.

You told them our relationship was never a physical one.

After that night when you lay resting waiting for me I went to my caravan. I had finished at Grays road and didn't know what else to do. I was in limbo.

The first thing I remember is the pigs raiding my van early one morning and being dragged off to prison.

When they charged me with the possession of that old firearm without a licence I was knocked for six. It didn't even work. They charged me with a lesser offence by mistake (Debbie G. was fit though; I nearly kissed her in the cop-shop). I rang my mum and step-dad. Keith wanted to know what on earth I was doing with a thing like that. I heard the Pigs shot round to tell you the good news.

You immediately assumed I was going to kill you. What do you really take me for? The Officers told me that I would get about eight or nine years in prison. I told my mum that I would rather die...I thought I would die, in prison.

It was like a hell on earth. I had to live with the kind of low-life scum I have avoided all my life.

I really didn't think I would be able to survive but my friends in Oxford supported me tremendously. They were instrumental in getting me through it and provided the Judge with some very good references.

The police tried to paint me in the very worse light possible.

The Judge told the Prosecution that they had to stop mentioning the other things they found unless they were going to charge me with them but they never did.

The Prosecution said that there were many more charges to come but they didn't actually materialize. There was a woman in the court who kept smiling at me who seemed vaguely familiar...

A small amount of cannabis in a bag, with a pipe (I had once experimented with Sarah (the manager of Headington library), who I had gone out with briefly after you. She came in and cooked me a meal for my birthday and really looked after me. I don't know what I would have done without her. (But I needed a much stronger personality).

A sacrificial dagger. Some liquid I had bought on the Internet without any serious intentions. I had money to burn in those days! What an idiot.

I received eighteen months for the time when Benji saw me closing the door.

I received two years for the firearm and bullets, but was told I would only serve half.

My Solicitor's Secretary said: "What do you think of that? You will be out in March." I was greatly relieved.

'

Two years in prison (and I <u>was forced to serve the full two years in prison</u>, even though I was released to a hostel at the half-way stage): for having a firearm I only had because I felt depressed.' It could only happen to me.

Those days in prison were the worse of my life and I've had some low points I can tell you. I felt you thinking about me when you held some of my artwork, and when you found my woolly hat. The one you all laughed at me wearing in Malta. The second jug wasn't as nice as the first one though. Its face wasn't as expressive.

I could also feel your mother's sadness despite what she might have said about allowing me into the house...

Shortly before I was released from prison a really nasty man, who was there on some very serious charges, attacked me from behind in a dark corridor, because he said I owed him a mars bar. It took me a while to get him down and restrain him, but by that time he had hit me with something in my face and blood was spurting all over the corridor and walls. One of the officers said she had never seen so much blood.

I was in a terrible state and made a mess in my trousers...

I nearly passed out.

I called the police in to press charges, and all they did was give him a 'caution.'

The Officers played tricks on me all the time. A lot of people went crazy in there.

You said in one of your statements that you thought you were going up-the-wall. You are lucky. You were barking already!

When I came out of prison they sent me to Milton Keynes.

They told me I couldn't talk to any women without their permission because I was so 'dangerous'.

I went to a beautician without telling them (I could have been recalled).

When I saw a woman up at the shops with the same mouth and nose as you it made me feel very sad. A year in prison was a very long time to me.

Roger gave me some book tokens he had just received for his birthday the day I was released and took me for a curry.

Do you remember Roger? You called him an 'anorak' when you first met him, then you said he was nice. I can't help but agree with you now.

When I came back from spending the book tokens the police were waiting for me, and tried to charge me with something I had not done. The CCTV in the book shop confirmed my story. When I eventually moved to a hostel in Norwich I was shocked to realize how much time had gone by. I was training to be a 'Spiritual healer' at a nearby church when I met a really pretty lady in her early thirties called <u>Cristina</u>. She had a First-class honours in literature, and could speak four languages fluently. She had grown up in Portugal but looked and sounded Swedish. I was extremely proud of her...They were due to recall me for walking her back to her car one night and for being ten minutes late, so I went on-the-run. I drove across to Ireland to pick up a caravan and then over to Banbury. I received a free membership at the gym after a few months. ~Eventually I came back to Wallingford. It all felt so surreal. I let myself in by the usual methods.

 You left a postcard from your holiday in the kitchen. I did wonder why your escort had signed it 'G.Mills.' Very formal. I don't know how I didn't wake you all slamming the door so hard.

The next time I went over you were in the kitchen for ages toying with your hair while you gabbed on the phone. I was getting very bored, and it was bluddy cold in that garden. The spikes on the wall were no deterrent; I flew over them!

It felt so strange seeing you Elizabeth. You'd hardly changed, but your hair looked a bit lighter. You were always asking people if they preferred blondes.

Benji and Emily came in and out of the room several times. I guess they were about ready for bed. Emily went to switch my telly and video off.

I don't know if I had been seen but Benji went to fetch your new lodger and got her to look out into the garden. He pointed but that was all. She went back upstairs. Then I saw you hide behind the door with a very mischievous grin, peeping round it, as they all went up to bed. You scolded them up to bed.

You plonked yourself down on your computer chair with a glass of wine in one hand and a bottle in the other.

You pretended to peer round the door, and then very naughtily shoved both hands into your trousers. You made some really suggestive faces as you looked at the screen. Unfortunately, I was unable to see what was on it in spite of standing in the corner with my binoculars. You simulated sex and appeared very raunchy.

You were wearing your tweed trousers and you had your glasses on. Your middle area looked a bit loose and paunchy.

Emily came to watch you and stood by your side. You nodded at the screen. She stood for a short while and then went out and shut the door...good for her! I was so sorry for you. I didn't know what to do. I have never seen anything so sad in all my life. I could have cried. I think I did shed a few tears watching you.

Your hand went in and out all the time. Sometimes you just lolled in a stupor. You appeared to be communicating with someone and typing with great difficulty and deliberation.

After a while your glasses fell off and you slumped in your chair, with your belly extended and your shirt sticking out.

You seemed to be slurring your speech.

Benji came down from upstairs. He sat on the couch behind you pretending to be asleep. He kept sneaking a look out into the garden (god knows how he knew I was there) and then back at you at what you were doing. You were masturbating in front of your own children! This went on for several minutes. He kept arching a bit closer and tried to peer over your shoulder to see what you were looking at.

You kept wafting your hand at him as if to say he had to stay put, and you couldn't help what you were doing.

I suppose he must have been about twelve by this time, although he still wasn't very tall.

Then he got up and went.

You spilt your wine.

Your trousers were split.

When you dropped your glasses you started to squint at the screen and your head tottered backwards and forwards.

Then you suddenly got up and went to bed.

Am I mad to think I should have been there with you in person?

I left Emily some presents, which I know she opened.

I felt uneasy the next week. As if someone were thinking about me. I thought it was the u-know-who's. I always have a sixth sense about filth.

Driving across I felt very troubled. I even passed a panda car leaving Didcot.

I parked my car up the road and walked down. The field and woods had changed a bit....I stood on a large tree-trunk on the other side of the road. The woods had been cleared.

When I reached the jumping wall I knew something was wrong. You were all huddled together on the sofa. You looked absolutely petrified and on the edge of breaking down. I am so sorry for that. I can never tell you how sorry.

I could not resist sending you a message as I stood in the corner on the spur of the moment. It was very foolish of me. I am very sorry for using the C-word. I meant to write hairy bush. It sounded very crude, and I never liked to be crude with you. That's when you tried to ring me. I saw you toying with a white pencil between your lips and looking for some details: probably the Eustace fellow's. It was the only sex-text I ever sent you.

You got the children upstairs, flicked the lights off, and went to lie on the back-hall floor peeking through the cat-flap. I hardly dared to breath. I knew if I were caught there I would be in serious trouble. I was surprised after what I had seen that you told anyone. I knew the cops had arrived but I couldn't move until you went upstairs.

I was only just able to get away as they came around the corner with a police dog.

I cut my hand scaling a seven-foot fence...Not bad for a geriatric!

I rang and said I was sorry and never meant to hurt you. Benji answered the phone. The policeman put on a funny voice pretending to be you. I could have left the area but it was cold and I didn't really know where to go.

I knew they were after me. When I was followed coming from the bike-shop the next day I knew my number was up.

They dragged me from my car even though I wanted to go peacefully. I was so petrified that I actually called for my mother.

I could hardly breathe and I thought they were going to kill me. They kept calling me the most repulsive names and thumping me because of you. They told me that if I ever returned to Oxfordshire they would; "hunt me down!"

You said in your statement that you had to go to the doctor because of me and that Benji had to too. I am sorry if I added to your problems but you were seeing the doctor long before me. You made it sound as if I was the source of all your problems. You blamed me for almost everything. You said you were afraid of what I would do next and that I might ruin your life...You said that you knew it was me who sent you the message because I was always sending you explicit messages, which wasn't true. You told the court that you were afraid I was going to commit a serious sexual offence against you, which as you probably knew was absolute rubbish. You told the court that you were afraid of appearing because you thought I might attack you...!

You told the court you didn't want to appear in person because you thought I might get too turned on if I heard your voice. I used to walk away from the phone sometimes because your voice was so boring and monotonous.

I don't know if anyone has ever told you, but prison is not a joke, and it isn't funny. When I received another sentence of two and half years it was a terrible shock. I received an extra year for not notifying the police of my 'change of address......!' Eustace grinned at me when I got the sentence. A woman in the dock was almost crying.... He bragged about visiting you forty or fifty times. He said the kids came running to see him. Probably just trying to make me jealous. He said he'd never seen a wine bottle anywhere.

I represented myself over the phone call business even though I was in such a terrible state and very out-of-sorts: no breakfast, no shower, and no sleep.

I was charged with contacting you on the phone (on my birthday)..."I'm sorry, but I never meant to hurt you!" How is that threatening? I was referring to the broken museum fire-arm which I had intended to end my life with, which was not about you. The Prosecution dredged up every horrid little detail they could from the past. They tried to make me look as bad as possible. It was very one-sided. They weren't interested that you still had some of my property, and they believed your statement that our relationship was never intimate, that you had only known me a few weeks, and that I had stalked you until you had to have psychiatric treatment and were in fear of your life.

I had to serve the remainder of the first sentence along with this new sentence, and also all the time I spent 'at-large'.

My former employers couldn't believe the severity of my sentence. Neither did they think I deserved the label given me by the police and the media thanks to you.

My second sentence was even worse than the first.

I don't know how I ever got through it. It completely wore me out.

I was attacked by someone suffering from schizophrenia in the middle of the night. It just seemed to go on and on forever. When I eventually got out I was <u>recalled for going on a library computer even though I didn't contact anyone I was told not</u> to and had to spend another humiliating and tortuous year inside.

I was sent to HMP ******* where I went on the main wing, but had urine and even more unpleasant things thrown through my door. Some of the young men said the most revolting things to me. They threatened to slash my throat and even tried to set fire to my cell. My mum never came in to see me. She said she had a toothache and that all sex-offenders should be castrated. Pam and Howard offered to drive over to see me every week. I couldn't help asking: what had I really done to deserve all this?

The police stopped me from going to my Writer's group and from attending the church. They warned everyone that I was a <u>*dangerous psychopath*</u> before I was released, and no doubt exaggerated everything I had done. They poked their noses into everything I did. I wasn't allowed to do anything without their say so. I wasn't allowed to make any meaningful friendships.

My sister and mother were told the most spiteful and prejudiced nonsense.

Just before I came out they applied for a SOPO order, because that was the end of my sentence, and I was not on the Sex offender's register. They applied for it just so they could keep tabs on me and so they could interfere in everything I did.

They told the court that I was in danger of attacking you or a member of the public and committing a serious sexual offence. They also labelled me as being a danger to children. When I stood up for myself and said that this was absolute nonsense and that we had split up because I didn't want to touch you I was accused of being aggressive.

The Magistrates peered down their snooty noses at me.

No doubt my goose had been cooked long before I even appeared in the dock. The Pigs were happy to see my name added to the ever-growing list of "wrong-uns." Having your name on the list gave them immediate access to your home and the power to have you thrown into prison quicker than a Politician knows how to run.

All they saw was my label and where I came from.

I totally reject this description of me.

I do apologise for not being able to tell you about all this in person

AND FOR MY POOR HANDWRITING...

ORIGINAL STORY WRITTEN 2009-11. Edited, tweaked, and up-dated January 2018.

Putting on Emily's shoes

In the morning, when you rub your eyes,
The door opens, And mummy calls:
"Hurry, or we'll be late!"
Our jeep lies purring in the driveway.
You sit above me on the stairs,
Your brown hair, Straight down by your sides,
You look at me, Without a whisper,
Waiting for something, Eating your biscuits.
I try to comb your strands,
But you shake them again, wilfully.
I hunt for your footwear among the bric-a-brac,
The assortment of toys and boxes…
One push and I'm sure it will be alright,
But your tiny feet seem far too big for the space…
So, I undo your straps and start once more,
In earnest,
Trying to persuade them in,
Coaxing them along,
And tie them gently…
Now you are free to stand,
And I can swing you up, high into my arms,
My Sweet Emily.

EARLY VERSION

ODE TO THE TROOPER 2

Peter Manion, you are bad,
Could have been a bigger lad,
Took your lass to meet your ma,
Taste the tongue of dear old da.

On the grass you sit and chat,
When she's had it .. her ass,
Until the morning lit your path,
You smoked a fag to celebrate.

Belinda's Hot air (Extracts from the World-famous Web-site)

Full Moon tonight!

By GODFREY WINKLEBACKER | Published: JANUARY 31, 2018 | Edit

I hope the chains are on all the main windows and doors in Downing Street.

SPROG By Brian 'Moon-dog' Spiggot February 2018

"Took Sophia to the Doc's today. Her ears were alright when we got there, but her throat is still very sore. Her constipation seems worse than ever!"

NORWICH CHARITY BOOKSHOP By Cedric Goodwise Muesli

"You can see it's a small book shop: that's why we don't allow anything too weird and I'm a skinny balding non-entity."

CHICKEN THIEF

Dorcus stole some chicken out of my bag last night but wouldn't admit it. She said she was nothing like; Brian, Sally or Margaret.

Jupiter falling

We came to an open patch of ground which was not dissimilar to the lower kingdom. It was surrounded by a fringe of beech and ash. A mist floated above the ridge. We could hear the distant sound of water. A feeling of peace descended on us all.

I opened our pack and handed round the flask. It had taken us four days to climb up to the plateau. I found the air warm and could smell the faint hint of honeysuckle. Just as the Sun came rumbling over the mountain we heard the clang of goat bells. As we walked into the centre of the meadow the noise of a mandolin gradually rose from the cliff face. Along the lip of the escarpment the ruins of a castle wall teetered into the distance.

A man began to appear up the coastal path. Beside him strolled the most magnificent golden lion.

Its mane blew in the breeze.

A white chair appeared through the mist, as if a curtain had been slowly raised before us.

When the stranger reached us, the lion bared its teeth. We could feel the heat of its breath. Even Eridor fell to his knees. The man raised the ivory branch in his hand and seated himself on the chair. The lion lay down at his feet. He had the deepest blue eyes I have ever seen and hair like the white of dawn. The man wore a toga of orange with a cloak of scarlet. Around his head there revolved a blue disc. Above the chair there appeared a crescent of seven stars, like a crown glowing with jewels. "*I am Landru*," he said, and bade us assemble before him. The Leaders were waiting in the valley below. Even our greatest scientists were unable to divert the peril approaching the planet. *Hygiea* was due to enter the atmosphere in exactly ten days time. Crowds of people were gathered in all the sacred places of the earth. Some were praying while others indulged themselves in rites to Bacchus. A mob of vigilantes were purging the prisons. Riots and lynch mobs wandered the streets. Antimagus came on the screen. He smiled at our small group with the generosity of a king. His black cape was wrapped tightly around him and he held on tightly to the wheel. "What has the renegade Landru replied?"

A new laser had been developed which could reach into the deepest regions of space. Without it the world would die and the whole history of mankind be wiped clean from the record.

"Remember all the treasures we have made. The great works of literature and art, gone forever!"

Landru looked down on us. He whispered into the ear of his priestess, but said nothing more.

"Everyone will die. Every living soul will be gone. Not a single animal will survive. The human race will be destroyed forever. All our discoveries and inventions will vanish for good. There will be no evidence we ever existed...the mountains will explode and our seas condense into space. The future will never know us."

Landru did not speak. He listened to our counsel and drank from a silver goblet. From the cloud above a raven flew down to his side.

"If the earth perishes, then so do you!"

"It is the fate of all living things to die, and so do men. I am More-than-man. What is death but a journey into the unknown. A total eclipse of the visible. That is all. Fear not oblivion. My race lived before the Universe grew dark. My soul will go on but the earth will no longer drink of it."

When we returned six days later there was a herd of small elephants feeding in the open. A lady in grey brushed the seeds on the ground. The little animals ran to her with their trunks outstretched and what seemed to be a feeling of joy. We loaded our weapons but did not fire at anyone. The plateau seemed saturated in a pale-yellow radiance. I thought I could hear music.

"The works of Shakespeare, Alexander, and Euripides. Have you not heard? Cervantes, Goethe and Grasse. Sapho's love poems. Our first spacecraft. The paintings of Red-beard, Picasso and Rothko. All will be spent. Never to be seen again. Extinguished, like the penultimate Rembrandt. Titian, Cezanne, Velazquez, and Raphael. Manet, Dali, Vermeer! Ulysses, Homer and Lewis. Lennon, Clapton and Orbison."

He turned his head and raised his brow.

"Gone forever!"

"Their time was done."

"Nothing remains forever... Not even memory when the

last body has decayed."
We returned with our bags and lit up our campfires. The injured were placed on a carpet of poppies. He cured them with his breath and by the power of his thoughts. The earth was still turning but the clouds seemed to race across the heavens like a rush of geese.

On our third visit to the meadow Landru did not appear. Instead we noticed a huge dragon-fly which circled around the outer rim, landing for a few seconds on the chair, before speeding off high into the mountains. When we went closer to the chair we saw the opaque outline of fantastic creatures. Eagles, falcons and dragons. After making oblations to the deities we made our way through a small gap in the trees and returned to our camp just before nightfall. I noticed a strange shape in the heavens. It was close to Jupiter and resembled a vast shifting morass. It felt then that the end was near.
We visited *Landru* just one more time. He appeared as before: slowly pacing up the cliff with his cane, but on this occasion, he was accompanied by a harp player whose face was hidden by their hood. Antimagus had taken poison and his craft was gone, into the depths of the soil. We pleaded with him to help us. We petitioned him to melt the menace from the sky. Elidor had been killed in the skirmish. Landru tended him with his voice.
He bade us rest and enjoy the wild deer of the forest.
"Who, or what are you?"
"A traveller!"

"We all travel. We are all travellers."

"My flight restores me to the place where I was formed. While the earth is consumed with fire my feet will walk again on the sands of my City. For I will have stepped through the door of eternity, which leads to *the plain of Valderama*."

"The time has come," he said. "For all men must die and so too the earth on which they live. There will be no others to succeed you or replant what you have lost."

"But what of Kant, Plato and Aristotle. Their names will never be heard again. No one will remember the land which was Earth. Our cities will die and all the creatures of the planet suffocate. Is that just? How can you let our entire civilization pass away and come to nothing?"

He waved his hand and left us.

"You fail to mention *natures' tyrants and monsters*. A hub of the world which you crave and whose actions will reverberate throughout the Hall of the Ages. All places have their monsters for what would life be without them?"

A JOURNEY INTO DARKNESS?

We first detected the *Parchments* entitled '***Thunderbuck Ram***' on the back of a Tinker's cart in the middle of the Gobi Desert, among a stack of foul smelling crubeens. How they got there from a builder's skip outside the Savoy I wouldn't really like to speculate. They were hidden inside a camel's hump and could easily have been lost forever. I had to exchange a few gold bars and seven photos of Marilyn Monroe for the pleasure of holding them. They appeared to be of great age, but then so does Hayley Mills. Most of them were in perfect physical condition, except for a few wine stains round the edges. We travelled home by way of the Nile and arrived back in a state of great confusion. Were the pages, as some experts suggested, a battle between the traditional polar opposites of 'good' and 'evil,' or were they simply the utterings of a mad-man who became possessed as a result of contact with demonic forces? A collection of the original work was known to be squirrelled away in the Vatican vaults but we were too scared to ask Pope Benedict XVI to see them in case he had a complete nervous breakdown. Copies were placed inside the porch of every church in the country in 1996 but many were taken by little green men or ravaged by beasts. Some were believed to be sold on the black-market. An advertisement asking for their return brought little response. The parchments do appear to contradict the early teachings of the church yet they begin with a very traditional view of right and wrong. A few damaged pages were discovered among the Archbishop's artefacts just after he collapsed doing press-ups on his house-keeper.

PARCHMENTS FOUND ON HILL

What do we discover in these sheets of misery, if not compassion and an insight into the mind of a socio-path? People who can't or don't want to spend time understanding someone will often label them or put them in a box...

At Ragnarok Loki will help to destroy the Aesir. Civilizations must come and go. Loki is certainly the rightful son of Woden. In ancient times the Sun was thought to die at night and to travel through the underworld, only to be reborn the very next day. Perhaps this tale of woe will one day bring light back to those who live in shadows...

Doctors and Nurses

By BIRD DUNG | Published: JANUARY 22, 2018 | *Edit*

1. No incentive to cure
2. A long list of maladies
3. Sex changes our priority
4. Free to all ticket holders
5. Trust me, I'm a quack
6. Unsustainable life expectancy
7. Lack of immediate consistency
8. Terrible lack of something
9. Richer pickings elsewhere

Groping essential for dirty old men

By HERPES ZOSTER | Published: JANUARY 24, 2018 | *Edit*

We hear today, at Bunderchook HQ, of shenanigans at the Dorchester Hotel. The venue for a children's charity for many a long year. Waitresses were 'forced' (under pain of poverty), to wear sexy revealing dresses, and stockings, to satisfy a revolting array of well-heeled and popular members of the Establishment. Some of the Waitresses even had their bottoms slapped or their tits groped. Imagine how it must have left them feeling? This can't go on! All donations must be returned at once or our society will never be able to live with the stigma.

- We condemn this behaviour absolutely
- It is truly shocking and unforgiveable
- It makes us very angry and annoyed
- Rug-munching feminists even more angry
- Could not restrain our anger any longer
- A man was observed trying to get his end away
- *An absolute monster attempted to take a phone number*
- Hard to ignore without getting a nose bleed
- Pissed ourselves laughing afterwards…
- Screwed up their life bending over a hobby-horse
- Will appear in Court for next to nothing
- Was left feeling humiliated and completely unsatisfied
- A victory for all decent minded citizens

*Satan must have been alive in their midst all the time for this kind of depravity to take place under their noses.

TODAY'S NEWS IN BRIEF

Prince William has just had a new hair-cut costing £150. This is a lot of money to some people. At least he is not trying to cover it up and has not invested in a harmful hair-transplant or a horse-hair-wig.

Fat-ass Didwell is still watching us at her window when we come in, in case we shut the door too hard and she can report us again.

Teen-age pupils are going to be reported by their teachers if they have any kind of sexual relationship while still at school.

Mum tried to get inside my bedroom three times last night, allegedly looking for "the cat?" It's a good job the door was heavily barricaded because the last time she tried to get in I was in the middle of having a .ank, and couldn't answer her straight away.

Harry-the-Gnome will no longer be able to poison the locals with malicious gossip. During the last few weeks he had become extremely yellow in appearance. He has gone to meet the great Cabinet-maker-in-the-sky.

Dorcus rang her son again to ask if she could fawn round her grand-daughter if she bought him another new organ.

Wayne Sleep is on the telly again. No wonder his knees are sore.

Corrie didn't win a single award last night. The amateur actors of Emmerdale were voted top, but then they are the gayest show in town.

Paul 'Dog-Rough' O'Grady and Count David 'Walliams' were both given awards for shit-stabbing and sucking up to the Producers.

A sample of piss was left at the Market Surgery Reception today. Enjoy!

<u>Sheree Brown</u> (probably an alias), a former member of my Writer's Circle has asked me to edit some of her short stories. They are tales she told her daughter many years ago to help her sleep. Sheree insists she is married yet still sends me text messages in the middle of the night, along with several kisses, to say she can't sleep and is suffering from anxiety. She is pretty fit to tell the truth, and has a very sexy face. I could show her my cock some time but it would have to be in a nice warm environment. I am due to meet her at the café in town soon. I had thought about confessing how I had failed to have any children of my own. I have been wondering for a while whether to ask her to 'put a bun in the oven' for me.

Doctor Gillam has bought a copy of my latest book edition (Thunderbuck Ram – Eye of the Medusa). I will have a lot of explaining to do if he gets the gist of it.

A middle-aged UKIP leader has been found guilty of shagging a good looking twenty-year-old chick. We are completely horrified!

TODAY'S WEATHER

Storm clouds will be followed by heavy showers. A high-pressure zone is expected to enter the Norfolk Broads before very long. Gale force winds coming from the West are due to lash the country for several hours. Snow may fall on higher ground with a scattering of sleet over the surrounding farmland.

ALL ABOUT BASEMA

Several years ago, while living and working in Oxford I became a close friend of a Syrian lady, who taught at a private girl's boarding school in Kuwait. While glancing through some old files yesterday I noticed a photo of her which I hadn't seen for ages. When she was twelve Basema sang at a birthday party for President Assad, who was a friend of her family. She sent me a video.

We became very intimate friends after meeting on *American Singles* and shared all our thoughts and aspirations. When ever we spoke I suddenly felt inspired to write her some poetry. It was as if a little bird suddenly started to sing in my heart. She began teaching me Arabic. I found it an easy language to learn. We spoke every day. She sent me many gifts and shared a lot of confidences with me.

After some time, she asked me to marry her. She wanted us to get married on the island of Cyprus and for me to convert to Islam. She was in her mid-thirties, but said that I was her *last chance* to settle down and have some children of her own.

I never doubted that her love was genuine, and that when I let her down and went away, it broke her heart.

I can't help feeling that she must have died. (**January 2018**)

UKIP leader found guilty of humping twenty-year-old

- ✓ Terrible
- ✓ Revolting
- ✓ Bad
- ✓ Sick
- ✓ We don't like him
- ✓ She's bloody fit!

She says 'you did it'

I spoke to Pain-in-the-butt on the phone last night. It was all I could do to end the call without a fight. She told me she had taken mum to the loo while they were in Norwich, and that mum had left something nasty on the seat.

"I wish you wouldn't tell me what mum says about me," she said. "She says a lot worse things about you!"

"Well, I don't take any notice of anything she says about you," I replied. "Just like you don't take any notice of anything she says about me…"

Me and my cock.

HUNTED

In line with Government policy the pigs are going to be given a huge boost to their budget so they can:

- Mount more cameras, on trees, pavements and Parkland
- Assess who is going in and out of Casualty without a parking permit
- Find out if Blacky the sheep has insurance cover
- Read brain waves from Outer space
- Discover if lepers have a chip on the shoulder
- Test for rabies and low I Q's
- Unearth crimes from the Hundred Years War

Respect!

WHO LIVES IN A HOUSE LIKE THIS?

left you a message

the funeral was cancelled until next week

I checked the car instead and put some fuel in

it needs some brake fluid   topped up with windscreen

when I got in mum demanded the keys
she said she wanted to go out in the car with Diane

when I told her it was best not to drive she called the police again
she called them yesterday too because they
suddenly turned up at the supermarket (over the same issue!)

fraid I had to give the keys back to her as she started smashing up
my room
I told her what you said about the Social Worker wanting me to do
the driving...

oh sorry, the room: according to Aunty Jenny she can do what
she likes because its her house>

the starting point for all this should always be:
1 sly ignorant family
2 lying little cow

mum says they are having another meeting about me
to confirm what a 'dangerous' man I am
more bullshit on the way then!
now do you see why I don't have anything to do with you all and keep out of the way
long discussion with mum after this mornings' events

and I am physically and emotionally drained

I had to tell her what you said about her state of mind
(or whatever is going on) but she slammed her door
and wouldn't listen...
She said you would be sorry!

I hope you don't mind me defending myself, afterall,
I have not used the car once for my own use since
it came back but only to run mum around

she has suddenly got all nice again now

Steam coming out of her ears!

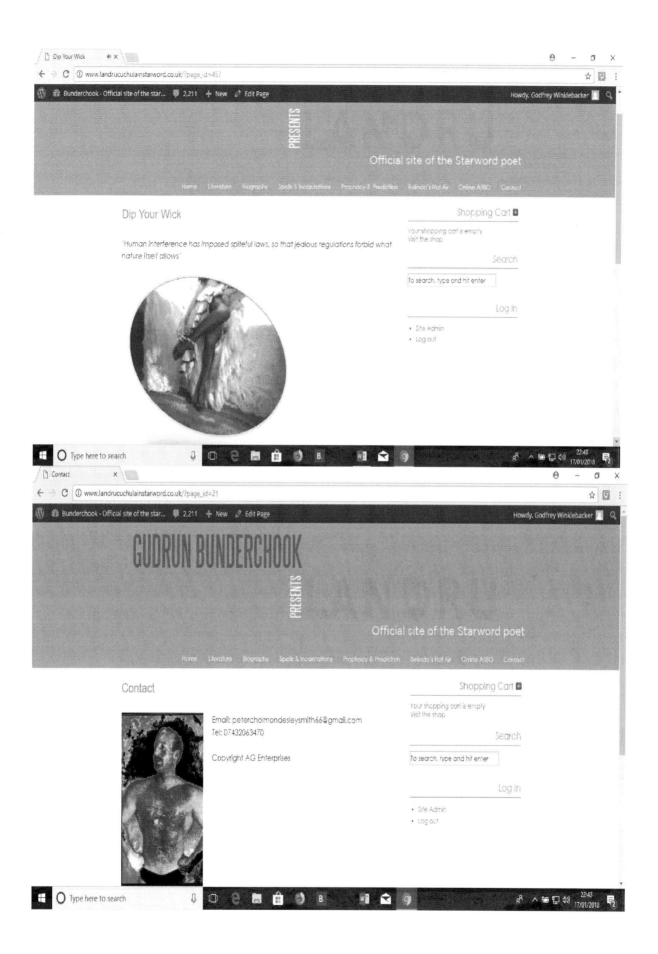

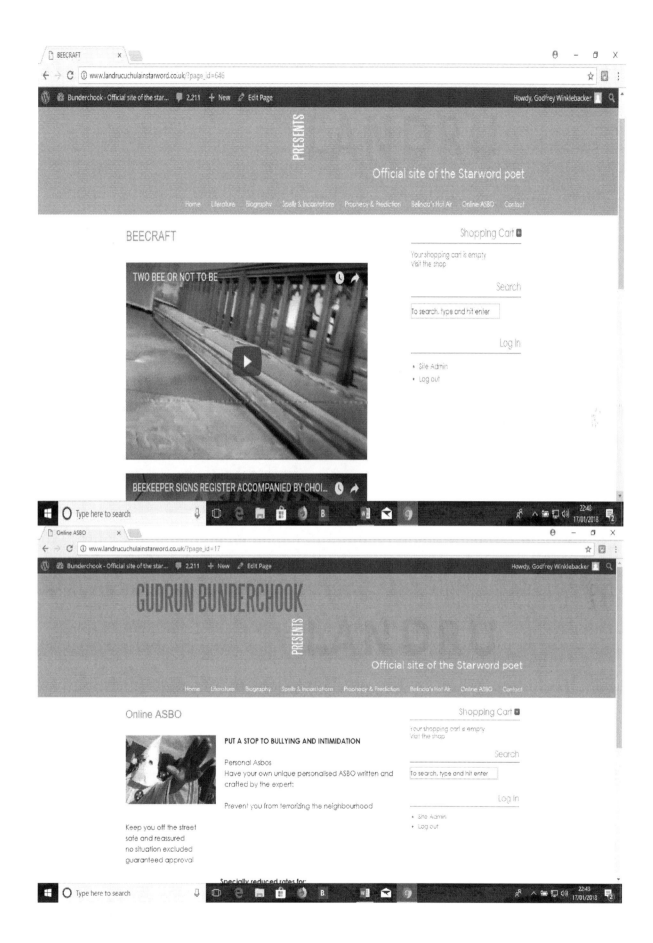

BACK TO NATURE.

The turns of Cedric Blatherskite

My brilliant career began in deck-chairs! Each summer I worked on the beach. For months I rented them out to the tourists who flocked to the coast. But then in winter my income dried-up. I had to resort to selling push-chairs and cuddly toys. Puppies were old-hat. I enjoyed a brief success with Hula-hoops, but only on week-days. Then I hit on a scheme which ultimately changed my life for the better.

I assembled a small horse from the debris I found on my beach-combing days. It was only little to begin with, but it grew fast, along with my intentions. Its body was long and brown. I nailed a tail on its rear, with real hair. It had teeth, probably plastic. I'd found a pair of old dentures under an ice-cream cone. By the time I'd finished its mane went all the way down its neck. I pulled the object along by means of a length of string. It finally rested on four wooden wheels, with a square bottom. The wheels were a bit rocky over hard ground, but with the right amount of effort I was able to get someone on board and drag them along on the sand.

I began by charging a penny-a-ride. The big girls were often too large and clumsy to get on properly, so I had to confine my propulsion to just the little ones. Within a remarkably short period of time I was having it away with many of them. Call it my Christian charity. I liked to do my good deed for the day. I liked doing a good turn for those around me!

As I led their offspring along the sands their parents would wave from the roadside. I was happy to see them so happy. It gave me a great sense of job fulfilment. I really felt as if my life had come to something.

The number of my customers can never be underestimated. They go beyond words. They can never be counted.

I banned swearing of course. Words like fuck, cunt, and cock, were never spoken while I was on duty. Dirty words, which had no place at all in our wonderful town.

For a small additional fee, the recipients were allowed to stroke the animal. I even provided a small pair of clippers and a brush to comb my Neddie's hair.

Many years passed, and I never put a foot wrong. My reputation snowballed. I was even put on the national news. Details of my exploits were spread all around the continent, until nearly everyone wanted a piece of the action.

Just before the tenth anniversary of my *announcement* I had to replace two of the wheels, which had broken off. My accountant listed this as 'operating costs.' You are bound to get a bit of wear and tear due to persistent usage.

Some of the parents lent me a hand. I had to have two whole days off work because of a bad back!

My popularity continued unabated. Occasionally, when asked, I would have to explain what the 'thing dangling between his legs was...'

"That is Neddie's fifth leg!" I would reply.

"He only needs it to give him a rest, when you've had your turn on the back."

BRITAIN'S FAVOURITE WA.KS

During my time with the Trust I ran a walking group for the disabled. Some of my group had been sectioned. Others suffered from a 'learning' disability, or were overweight. I was surprised how often a truly memorable walk was hidden behind a busy and insanitary thorough-fare. One of my favourite walks took us to Bronte Water Falls. I was therefore delighted to see it among one of 'Britain's Favourite Walks,' a collection of the top hundred walks in the country.

Aged fifteen we returned from our Eagle Adventure holiday, organised by the YHA, along the wonderful Ingleton falls, which led into the village. Ingleton has to be one of the loveliest places in the world. I recall sitting in the café there many times, with my buddy Andrew Ducket, who was not a bit shy, but definitely a 'babe-magnet.' Though highly-placed, Ingleton did not quite reach the giddy heights of third place, which I correctly predicted might be given to Malham cove and Gordale scar. An atmospheric treasure trove which took you right back into prehistoric times and a place where we lost our Timmy chasing sheep.

Glencoe came in high as well. I once cycled from Fort William, through the Bridge of Orchy, and over Rannoch Moor. I was astonished not to see more of Northern Ireland on the list, but Devon was well represented.

Top of the list came the trek up Helvellyn and Striding Edge. Julia Bradbury was stunned to see it in first place. When I first climbed Helvellyn in my teens the summit was shrouded in mist. We had been sitting down among some rocks to rest and eat our lunch.

Our group contained an eighteen-year-old youth called Malcolm. He was a bit older than us and had a much stronger physique. His father was a bobby, so that may explain his manifest aggressiveness to us younger boys. I usually stood up to the bullies but he was not afraid to give you a kick.

A small boy called Peter ambled along in the rear. He was very frail, with blonde hair, and a had very quiet disposition. I noted how Malcolm strolled behind him tripping him up from time to time during the week.

We were all given the choice to march across Striding Edge. Most of us did it, but Peter was too nervous.

On the way back to the other side I followed Malcolm, who was wearing a white polo-necked shirt and green bomber jacket, and who was just in front of me. I was in last position.

Just as he was turning to say something I hooked my foot round his ankle. I think he said..." you little twat!" or something like that, before losing his footing and skidding over the mountain side. I heard his voice echoing down the rock face with the occasional jolt or scree slide in between. That was in 1971. I find it very hard to remember anything more. We just kept walking on as if nothing had happened.

Chris, our leader, asked where he was when we got back to the youth hostel.

"I think he went home. He thought it was all too boring."

The End

DOING OUR BIT FOR SOCIETY

October 2018

Hi Sue, and Bob too,

Just a few things to say about Thursday's meeting. I am reluctant to come along if it's going to be about labelling me again, but then you seem to have already done that, or there wouldn't be a meeting...

I'm sorry to hear Annie can no longer be there because she needs to be with her grandchildren. You can never be too careful these days.

So, I was wrong. Vicky will be there. I thought she would, because she is so interested in Africa and the plight of women. Doesn't news get around quick.

The Quakers are a Society of Friends for all. I wonder what Jesus would make of it?

Whose idea was it to have the meeting? I think this has a lot to do with what Bob found in my writing. The fact that I had a past. Over and done with years ago you might think...

but then, people are what they are.

I feel a bit concerned that he has gone sneaking off to the Authorities about me but what can you expect from people with such fixed and dogmatic opinions of right and wrong. This was after you both went running to the Vicar to see what he could add to the stereo-typing.

I knew there was something going on when I saw Anne's shifty looks towards me and the fact she bought the books so secretively.

At the moment I feel a bit as if I am being *put on trial*. Would you like to tell me what I've done wrong?

As I've already said. You are perfectly safe to sit next to me without any fear of exposure.

Since you asked:

1 I come to the meetings for peace and tranquillity

2 To talk to Clive

You asked me what I could give to the Quakers?

Quite apart from my wit and good sense of humour I could leave you my entire life savings but I doubt if that would be enough to stave off any prejudice.

To the Quackers

1 You were very quick to defend the police when I criticized them. Someone who looks up to authority would do that yet the police gang lie all the time. You said I was 'labelling' the police, but in their case, it happens to be true.

2 You wanted to meet me to alleviate any concerns you had. What are your concerns precisely, and why do you have them?

3 I would like to move on from the past, not to be reminded of it all the time. Do you think that's possible? Isn't there a certain amount of prejudice based on what you don't really know about me. Isn't this still all about labelling?

4 You spoke to me last meeting as if I needed support. Talking to friends would surely help, but this should be in a supportive and non-controlling way?

5 You mentioned me having to provide you with information about what I had been doing. Why should this be of concern to you?

6 What would Jesus have said about what you are doing. Jesus had a lot of trouble with backstabbers in authority too.

HI Sue

It was good to see you at the meeting this morning. I'm sorry I didn't stay for long. I don't really like business meetings and I was getting sick of Vicky coming to sit next to me in the hope that I would somehow reveal myself. I was able to make the stairs alright and had a chat with good old Clive.
I had a dream last night in which Will was stood in front of me. He was probably trying to tell me not to trust any of you. The Presbyterians know how to deal with turn-coats.

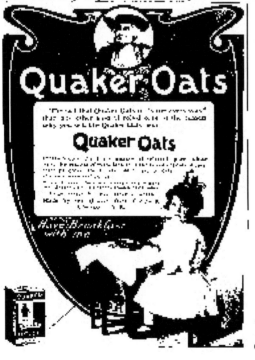

Scrags

Hi Rishikesh.

1 I just sent you an e mail with a few more points concerning this matter.

2 I have conducted a search like you suggested and it is still not there.

Believe me. I know what is going on here! The book has been deliberately scuppered
and is no longer among the Author's works, even though an earlier version is.
Someone in the town has made a malicious complaint to try and get the book removed.
I would like to get it re-instated, or at the very least get the offending 'adult item' deleted.
Please, let's get this sorted out properly as soon as possible. I know people who are very
interested in buying a copy but aren't able to find it.
Why should these rogues be able to make a complaint without any chance of an explanation?
If I knew EXACTLY what they were complaining about I could look at getting it removed.

Hi Samuel

Its a pleasure to hear from you. A lady I know has read this book and she makes no mention of any
adult material. I'm sure whatever the problem is it can be rectified. I could have a word with the
Author about getting it changed. I know a local Vicar who took offence at the book because it
contained a reference to masturbation.   I thought we lived in a more permissive age now. This would
surely amount to censorship. Besides, there are many worse things in books on the market these
days. In the classification it already says that the book contained 'adult material,' of a very mild sort.

Could you possibly find out **exactly what the adult item/s are,** the exact parts which have been
identified as toxic?

I am quite happy for you to share my thoughts with any senior Managers or Owners.

The strange thing is, after much searching I was able to locate and order a copy. I would just like to
know why it is being hidden from everyone else?

PAIN-IN-THE-BUTT

1 I wasn't 'walking around with a grin on my face'. I was in the next room.

2 I don't know anything about a £4000 necklace. Saying I sold it at a car boot sale is absolute bunkum.

If she goes around saying these things to the Watsons it will only give them more ammunition.

They believe it, because they want to believe it.

3 I have not been *bound over to keep the peace.* That night she went to the neighbours after

repeatedly trying to force her way into my room was about a year and a half ago now.

We have not had anything approaching that since. What's this about you going to the pigs yourself?

Contrary to what she said mum appeared very cheerful and up-beat. I heard her say to someone

on the phone not an hour ago:

"Andrew only needs to put one more foot wrong and he will be locked up in prison for life."

Vice and Queries in the House of Correction

I have been invited to have my opinions dissected and my brain screwed over by the Establishment. The Elders simply want to know:

1 What I would like from them

2 What I can give to them

3 Do I intend to get my cock out in any of the meetings

Look, folks. I don't want anything from you, except to be left alone. To sit quietly and un-molested. Just who will be my Inquisitors?

Will I be allowed to defend myself without being made to feel like a *real cunt?*

- ✓ Be silent! Button your lip young fiend. Do you know you are in the presence of the Lord? Everyone needs to have friends!
- ✓ "My name is Jean. I'm here to welcome you."
- ✓ "We have a shared responsibility to worship"
- ✓ "*Words* can break and disturb God's presence"

Which would *you* rather ride?

October 2018

Dear Work and Pensions,

I am writing to you about my recent assessment in which I was
moved into the support group. I am not sure of all the
different group names, but I feel sure that there are strong
reasons to appeal against this recent decision.

I did attend my first face-to-face meeting in North Walsham as
requested, but the trip made me very ill and I was bed-bound
for a whole day afterwards. My walking and balance is worse
in the morning, when I can be very un-co-ordinated and slow.
This problem seems to be getting worse. The interviewer seemed
more interested in talking to her boyfriend, who rang during
the interview, than she did talking to me. I found it very
difficult to get across town, even with my walking-stick. I
got very distressed and unable to cope. I often start
shouting at myself for the tiniest things. I am getting less
able to cope with people and social situations. My speech
seems to get a bit slurred. I have noticed that I am
dribbling from the left corner of my mouth sometimes. The
area round my mouth feels a bit numb. My writing has
deteriorated significantly; I am getting my letters jumbled up
and become angry when my hand won't do what I tell it. I
often forget things or make mistakes. The surgeon has offered
me a knee-replacement, but I am a bit worried about the
operation. My knees and joints have been so painful during
the last few weeks I have been unable to sleep or get
comfortable. I take a pain-killer or Voltarol, but it doesn't
really stop it. I am due to see my Doctor (Doctor Gillam) at
the Market Surgery here in Aylsham on the 22nd of this month to
discuss a whole host of problems, including the fact that I
was planning to kill myself. I may need a hip-replacement too.
I served five years in prison for having a fire arm which
didn't work and for contacting an ex-partner when I had been
asked not to. During my time in prison I remember being
attacked on more than one occasion and suffering head
injuries. I had been getting headaches for some time but this
experience has made it a lot worse. I often have bad dreams
about it all. When I do start to feel bad it can last for many
days, and it makes me feel as if I am actually dying. I have
called the ambulance more than once because of it.

I have suffered continuous name-calling by everyone and

harassment from the police over a number of years. My doctor
thinks that I will always suffer from 'anxiety.' He has said
this to me. I did try to write a book about my experiences but
the police/pigs tried to get it taken out of circulation. I
tried to do a stall in the market hall but I cannot carry the
things up the steps any longer. As I approach my 64th year and
see myself slowly deteriorating I do not see much future for
myself in regular *paid* employment.

I hope you do not mind me being so frank about my life. It is
true that I am not under a Psychiatrist or a Probation
Officer, although the police are always raiding where I live.
I am not on any cancer drugs or anything like that. I do have
a sleep condition which needs Zopiclone most nights. I had
been taking Amitriptyline for depression (twice) but it was
turning me into a zombie. I still have some if I need them.

I was ousted by the police and housing association from where
I was living because they said I was a 'Sex-offender,' and the
neighbours didn't like it. I was forced to go and live with
my mum who is getting dementia and can be very difficult. I
am just about coping with making our meals and keeping the
house clean.

My sister has told my mum that she must get rid of me as soon
as possible because they don't want anything to do with me,
but that would leave me homeless again. Everywhere I go I am
shunned by people and made to feel rejected. I did have a
girlfriend for seven years but the Housing Association put
pressure on her the whole time and told her that if she did
not break up with me they would evict her from her bungalow.
I do not have any money or savings, except what I get from you
and a small pension (which is deducted) from when I worked in
the Health Service. You will turn down my appeal I know,
because you say I say I can walk fifty yards without stopping.

Good grief: the pea-cocks are here

By RUMPLESTILTSKIN | *Published: OCTOBER 17, 2018* | *Edit*

Aunt and Uncle have just appeared at the door. I offered them a cup of tea after their long drive but they wanted to make it themselves. Neither of them spoke a word to me. I'd love to know what they think I have done to them. Mum has become her usual bossy self since they arrived and is itching for a fight.

Learning to play the flute with Rami

By RUMPLESTILTSKIN | *Published: OCTOBER 15, 2018* | *Edit*

I have begun to play the Native American flute. Robert dropped out because he is poorly and his fingers are a bit stiff. I have met a retired mental-health nurse there. When we were lying on the floor in the relaxation group I noticed how cuddly she looked lying there in front of me.

What are Friends for…

By HERPES ZOSTER | *Published: OCTOBER 6, 2018* | *Edit*

We've had a quick gander through one of your books to satisfy our prejudices. We've decided not to make any comment concerning any of the more important aspects of your writing. Instead, we are going to focus on whether we can recognise any local characters in there. It is crucial that we make this the centre of our witch-hunt.

It all falls into place…

By BIRD DUNG | *Published: OCTOBER 6, 2018* | *Edit*

Woman buys books for 'friend' in 'Sheringham.'
(She seems an unlikely reader of the genre).
Friend grills me on what he's found in them.
Hey presto! We have you.

Scots Quaker oats

By GODFREY WINKLEBACKER | *Published: OCTOBER 5, 2018* | *Edit*

The best cereal money can buy!

Getting in on the act

By ADUMLA | *Published: OCTOBER 5, 2018* | *Edit*

Is it any wonder that so many film stars and celebrities are claiming they were abused decades ago when the publicity is so rewarding…!

ESSAY TITLES

Talking cock seduces virgin bride

Man burns church at stake

Mother daughter relationship warning

Shake me at night like a warped door which rattles the teeth in my mouth

I love working for the church

By ADUMLA | *Published: OCTOBER 5, 2018* | *Edit*

One of my greatest supporters works at the church down the road. I have done everything I can to please him and his dog-collar.

- Provided him with many subjects for debate
- Given him plenty of time to question his faith
- Offered him occasions to cover himself in glory
- deliberated with him about the use of crystal balls
- Tested him on passages from the bible
- Been his staunchest ally at the Mother's Union

Trump doing all he can to stand up to Chinese and Russian aggression

By SURLOIN STEAK | *Published: OCTOBER 5, 2018* | *Edit*

But stabbed in the back at home by petty minded Democrats.

Red-wings horse and donkey gulag

By SURLOIN STEAK | *Published: OCTOBER 5, 2018* | *Edit*

1 You are not allowed to feed the animals

2 You aren't allowed to bring your bike in

3 Do not attempt to fool us with a plastic carrot

A change of name

By SURLOIN STEAK | *Published: OCTOBER 4, 2018* | *Edit*

I am changing mum's name.

She needs to be changed.

I had thought of F O, because she keeps coming to my door and hanging around outside my bedroom window.

Finally I decided on 'FOE.'

E stands for 'eventually.'

I entered the church tonight

By SARIN | *Published: OCTOBER 25, 2018* | *Edit*

To attend the third lecture on EVOLUTION.

When I first walked in Andrew was on his mobile phone at the back. I fear he may have been calling in auxiliaries. I asked the Professor why the church was always so antagonistic whenever any new theory came along. Look at the way it tried to belittle Darwin and make a fool out of him. Why was it so threatened? Was it because it feared losing much of its power and control over the people…As I turned to leave a tall imposing man lurking behind me glared towards me and followed me to the door.

Red-Wings

By PETER SMITH | *Published: SEPTEMBER 30, 2018* | *Edit*

I went to sponsor a donkey today. I decided to sponsor **Wiggins and Whacko** who were abandoned in a livery stable a few years ago. Apparently, donkeys can die of loneliness and need constant companionship. As I was making my way up the field a member of staff with a phone chased after me:

"Oh, no, you can't feed them!" she cried. "You'll have to give your bag of carrots to me!"

A police helicopter circled overhead.

Scheming pigs

By BIRD DUNG | *Published: OCTOBER 29, 2018* | *Edit*

Christine was sent to spy on me at the Town hall today. She loitered round the cards in the market-place and kept sneaking a glance into the passage-way, before dragging her shopping trolley in and going to sit at the tables. She didn't buy anything but looked over at me. She did not speak. Neither did I, you brainless oat-heads. Nice try, but we are not all as thick as pig-shit.

Feet up on the wall

With legs lifted you lay your head back,

The tardy paint of the bathroom blue,

Pressed against your feet,

And the ceiling above,

White as snow your pearl perfect velvet,

Long and slender, we moulded each other.

With arms around you, so tender,

You drank in my air,

Caressed my hands, and kissed them

Again and again,

With the candles flickering,

And the faint smell of lavender.

As I stand with the hoodies outside Tesco's,

Unlocking my bike,

You turn with your trolley,

Your lips quivering,

Your heart racing,

Without a murmur,

And walk to your car.

The skulls of Dalriada

'Are, like hardened rocks of salt,
Empty towns of the vanquished,
Sons who come no more.

Bread which has been broken,
A charnel cake of dew,
Fallen from the highest cloud,
A flurry filled with blue...'

If I could call on Prophets from,
The ages that are past,
And learn from those who would,
Give up their lives for faithless men,
I'd bring a shield, a cloak of oak,
The riches of the Branch,
And sing until the dawn arrived,
With sunlight from East.

I'd be a king, among the spent,
But yet, alive in song,
And you would hear my,
Words each spring,
Whistling on the wind.

Dear Team, Sue and Bob too

Just a few words about the circumstances which led you to talk to me.

You based your assumptions on something you had read in a book? Then you went off to talk to Andrew Beane about me. I wasn't trying to hide anything in my words. There are a lot of quirky things in there, for sure, but don't you think that telling the truth is important. Why should I hide any of it, or edit it out. Why focus on one small part when there are a lot of other less candid pieces in there? I'd like to do everyone a good turn if I can.

I'm presuming that you are only going on what you had read, but of course there are several ways you may have jumped to conclusions about me. Andrew may be a 'good Vicar,' but he is still human and, like all of us, can make mistakes. I noticed that a lot of the most high-profile people at his church were also the biggest gossips and back-stabbers. That isn't Christian. How is that modelling God's love and truth in the world?

You started by saying I had been banned from the Anglian Church. Would someone like to tell me why? (I haven't as far as I know!). No-one has said anything to me about it. I haven't gone there, not because I have done anything wrong, but because I wanted to avoid seeing my ex, who was bullied and threatened for seven years for being with me. I was a little dismayed by Andrew's attitude. It was quite obvious that someone must have been spreading stories to him too. All this is very behind-closed-doors and so you never really get to the full truth. It's all very one-sided and superficial.

As members of the Establishment I quite understand why you would want to side with Authority. An important reason why I write is to question this very Authority. As you probably know, people in authority lie a lot of the time, and so they need to be challenged. A lot of my views are probably very different to yours, but then the world is a big place. There's space in it for more than one opinion? I came to the meetings to experience a place of peace and spiritual contemplation. A refuge. The social aspect is just a pleasant bi-product. Its also helpful sometimes to have a few genuine friends. You also mentioned wanting to know what my activities were each day. Why would you want to know that. Why would you want to 'monitor' me unless it was to pass on information to someone else? This is really about *control*. I contacted my ex partner about nine years ago. This was over and done with a long time ago. The last thing I need is yet more labelling and stereo-typing. I don't want to go along to a meeting where once again, <u>men</u> are being victimised and put in a pigeon hole. There's always going to be one group of people telling another group of people how to live their lives, because they think they know best. I don't need 'treatment,' or 'managing.' This is the sort of attitude which comes straight from the Establishment. (I wouldn't try to force my beliefs on you, so why should you want to force yours on me). If we are all so equal then why am I being treated so differently? (Let's be specific!). I know prejudice is rife in town. If people would lay their prejudices down on the table we might be able to get somewhere.

I answered your queries quite fully when we met, so why weren't you satisfied with my elucidation?

Peace and friendship

DOLLY

Dear David *Editor,*

I hope you don't mind me writing to you about a recent 'advertising' article entitled:

'Local Author learns to leave the past behind,'

which appeared in Saturday's (29th September) Eastern Daily Press.
It was quite expensive once you had added the VAT. I was quoted £550, but a further £110 was added. A lot of money to a struggling Author like me.

I tried to get in touch with some of your Editors, because the story high-lighted a lot of sensitive subjects:

- Men's issues
- Depression and suicidal thoughts
- Harassment and intimidation
- Media bias
- Problems within the legal system

I did not even receive a single return call. Surely, articles like this, not only 'help' to sell your newspaper but they also raise matters of genuine concern to us all. In other words, the story deserved to be there on its own merits.

Another problem which I have become aware of: because the article is labelled as an 'advertising feature,' it is not freely available on-line to members of the public. This reduces its potential audience and robs people of the chance to learn something new. My friends living abroad are unable to get a link to the page.

I can see how this might be a unique case though.

I was pleased to see, however, that my feature linked well with other pieces on the day.

NO REPLY DUE TO FEAR OF LABELLING.

Brett Kavanaugh's sex accuser

By GODFREY WINKLEBACKER | Published: SEPTEMBER 28, 2018 | Edit

Says: 'I'm glad to get it all off my chest. Hilary's a very sore loser!'

Snitching off to Andrew Bean…

By PETER SMITH | Published: SEPTEMBER 23, 2018 | Edit

The Elders at the church have gone snitching off to the Vicar clutching my book between their legs. I was called into a meeting:
"We've read what you wrote, and now we want *to help you*, just in case you might want to murder one of us. You're a great writer, BUT A LOUSY EDITOR!"

Great news!

By SURLOIN STEAK | Published: SEPTEMBER 23, 2018 | Edit

The Quakers are going to label me as well.

That's it! Stick the boot in fellas.

The slaughter of Jamal Khashoggi

By USULI TWELVES | Published: OCTOBER 20, 2018 | Edit

I heard he hightailed it into the Embassy because his shoes needed shining and he was itching for a showdown. These journalists can really make life uncomfortable. We've looked everywhere but all we can find are a few bloodied hankies and a box of confetti. The British Government are furious and so are the United States, at least on camera. Gone are the days when *they* bumped off a rival or got rid of someone they didn't like because of the stories they had ON THEM…

Disgrace at Luton airport

By <u>SURLOIN STEAK</u> | *Published: NOVEMBER 2, 2018* | *<u>Edit</u>*

Today, a successful British athlete had to drag himself across the airport:

- wheelchair of poor quality and design
- a regular reader of 'the Independent'
- may have got a pressure sore on his BACKSIDE
- legs wouldn't work properly due to cough
- needed the publicity for his memoirs
- petulant and spoilt due to changes in public attitude
- wants to be the next dictator of the CUNTRY

Come join the British legion

By <u>ADUMLA</u> | *Published: OCTOBER 22, 2018* | *<u>Edit</u>*

I joined the British legion club tonight so I could play in the Chess club up-stairs.
The bar-girl was very friendly; "what can I get you young man?"
A drink for yourself, maybe?
After winning my first game I jumped into the air and shouted "Victory!" before racing round the room a few times, laughing and slapping the table.
My opponent, a much older wiser man resembling Vince Cable, was very reserved and hushed. I have trouble walking so I hobbled to the stairs.
As I came through the bar almost the entire village was waiting for me.
I opened the outside door, turned round and bowed at everyone there…

More police lies and corruption

By <u>GODFREY WINKLEBACKER</u> | *Published: OCTOBER 22, 2018* | *<u>Edit</u>*

The harm Julian Cole suffered at the hands of the British police can never be reversed. Unlike their notes, and the pack of lies they wrote to cover up their misdeeds. How come it took so long to get to the truth? Because so many people in our society suck up to these wolves, including our Politicians, priests and Civil dignitaries we are meant to respect.

More funds needed for health

By <u>ADUMLA</u> | *Published: OCTOBER 24, 2018* | *<u>Edit</u>*

A massive amount of cash was needed recently to repair the spine of some babies still in the womb.
Doctors. Medical staff. Hospital Administrators and Porters.
I am predicting yet more operations on 'foetuses' to prevent the Health Service from running out of patients.
Its a disgrace that any baby is born impaired or without the full array of equipment.

'It's what you accomplish in your life, not how old you live to be'

Forgive me for asking…Clive

By USULI TWELVES | Published: OCTOBER 21, 2018 | Edit

Just to put my mind at rest dear chap…
Have you offered to see me because of
Thursday's meeting, or not?
I do know how controlling these people
can be. You were right about Goethe,
by the way. If anyone in my town had
thrown plates out of the window they
would have been:
1 arrested
2 murdered
or
3 placed in a lunatic asylum

You're a kind man Clive. Have a documentary about Goethe on behind me. Eventually he rejected Christianity, I think, although he was greatly influenced by his Lutheran education. I can get a bit paranoid, I'm afraid. I try not to make any 'moral' judgements about people, although I quite understand that a lot of people at the Friends do.

They wanted to see me to discuss my future there, I believe. Am going to be interviewed by Bob, Vicky with the strange eyes, and Sue. If I do go along I hope I don't start arguing with them. I can defend myself, which is normal. If you are not careful, under those circumstances, it can become a bit like three against one. I am almost sure that Vicky has 'issues...' especially with white Englishmen.

The only real piece of feed-back I've had so far on my article was from a man at the library who asked me if I was some kind of Philosopher. He's never spoken to me since. I asked Bob if he had ever wound-up a member of the Establishment…a bit like shooting yourself in the foot I suspect.

He didn't answer, although he did say he was not a Member of the Establishment, which doesn't seem possible. Not to worry! I have a few Writer friends here and there, although not as many as I would like. We sometimes say how writing is our soul reason for living and without it we would die.

Not yet though! Would you like the *four feathers* sent round now or would you rather wait…

On the meeting. Can I get back to you on that? Let's make it pretty soon. Next century maybe?

WHY HATE THE QUACKERS

Mankind is an egotistical little prick.

It's always nice to hear from you Clive.
I'd never heard that story about Goethe before.
I mentioned in conversation a while back that you said you'd like to meet up
Sometime, but Anne said you had said that to *her* once...
I wonder what Vicky makes of me?? She likes to be in command.
You know what we were saying about people being labelled as one thing or another.
We seem to be on the same wave-length which is very reassuring.
I am doing another book-signing that day though and it happens to be in
the morning. Another time would be great.
I was going to mention something to you this morning but never got around to it.
It's rather a delicate matter, perhaps. But we are both men of the world!
Did you happen to see or did anyone mention a half page article in
The Eastern Daily Press (Saturday 19th September I believe).
Now, I know I have not been perfect in my life, and I have done some silly things
but I believe I am a fundamentally honest person and good at heart. I thought
of doing the article to clear the air, so that people could understand a bit more
about me. I had to cut a few corners, but it was, most of all, truthful, and I would
rather people know the truth than something which was made up.
Most people would shirk at the prospect but I am unafraid of popular opinion.
It would certainly be nice to meet up sometime. I have taken my mum, who
is acting increasingly bizarre, up to that Garden Centre. It is nice and quiet.
The deaf lady does a good meal there. I find Purdy's a bit too crowded and the Grimsey
Works in there. The other place I quite like is Biddy's, in the corner of the Market Place.
I like going to the meeting because it is quiet and tranquil, however some of the
Elders have taken it into their heads that I need some support after running off
to the Vicar in town. Someone has reported two of my books
(it just so happens to be the two books which Anne bought on Bob's behalf...)
and Bob was very judgemental in his approach to what was in them. They did
not focus on all the good writing but on one or two awkward bits which I have no
reason to hide. No matter! It will all come out in the wash as they say.

Peace and blessings

The freedom to speak

By SARIN | Published: OCTOBER 26, 2018 | Edit

A citizen of this town said to me a while ago that she had heard I was seen streaking through the town centre scaring all the Old-age Pensioners. I replied that I had never done so and never intended to do so in the future. I have a good idea who has been putting these rumours around town. Am I to remain quiet and not say anything at all against any of my persecutors? Do I have the right to defend myself. Am I right to speak out against the people who have been spreading this malicious nonsense? Is it wrong of me to replace their lies with the truth? Perhaps they were only having a laugh. I wish they'd say so.
Throughout history Writers have been suppressed and punished for speaking out against the tyranny of the State. Should those Writers not have their say because it may hurt the feelings of others? The very people who would put them into chains, given the chance.
A Writer is a solitary being, but a mob can have hundreds of animals in it.
To speak the truth without fear of persecution. To have a sense of humour and magnanimity where none is given. To speak out against the gossip mongers and tittle-tattlers.
I suppose it all depends whose side you are on...doesn't it?

Sir Philip Green Monster

By GODFREY WINKLEBACKER | Published: OCTOBER 26, 2018 | Edit

"Consistently rude to everyone!"

To everyone? To the wonderful human species. The Dictators and control-freaks. The moral do-gooders and wise-men of Kenya??

Oh, my goodness. Surely, this can't be right. I must be getting my facts wrong. And as Mr Green said, hiding behind Parliamentary privilege to make yourself popular is really undermining the law. I like the way this little man stands up for himself and isn't intimidated by the creeping subterranean palace bunnies.

"Are you lookn at me. Are ya?"

Gate keeper

By SURLOIN STEAK | Published: OCTOBER 29, 2018 | Edit

Gladis called round to see me at the book-signing today. It came into my head to mention the Gate-keeper, who I thought was somewhat stand-off-ish whenever I have been in her presence.

"Oh, she's just shy," barked Gladis. "She's a complete brain-box. You ought to see the qualifications she's got."

"Shy," I said, "the woman's nearly sixty. She can speak if she wants to. She chooses not to. I have seen her blush and occasionally snigger in my direction." This is a *dead parrot!*

"If you knew her you would understand," smiled Gladis.

"I do know her," I said. "And that's why I know how aloof and controlling she is."

"That's ABSOLUTE RUBBISH!" screamed Gladis down her mega-phone.

Hubble bubble toil and trouble

By SURLOIN STEAK | Published: OCTOBER 27, 2018 | Edit

I have promised some friends that anything we say or discuss in private will not be repeated by me on-line, and I intend to keep my word. Nor will I discuss any activities or conversations we have together in a bond of friendship.

Dear Shiela,

Thanks for your help the other day and for your efforts to bring us closer together. Please tell me this. Vicky studied literature and knows I write, but not once has she asked me about it or wanted to talk about books. Oh, well. Must have her reasons. I hope your little holiday goes well. We will miss you!

PEACE AND BLESSINGS,

Cure for an unsound mind

By HERPES ZOSTER | Published: NOVEMBER 1, 2018 | Edit

After years of research we have finally discovered a remedy for sickness. Trappers from the Siberian forest have passed on their ancient remedy. They advise that the tooth of a tiger or bear be placed into the head of the sufferer. It will cure anything from fits to complete paranoia. The best way to do this, apart from opening up the skull, is to push the object in through a nostril or ear-hole. It should be left there indefinitely until a significant improvement can be observed.

Secret agent Gladstone

By <u>GODFREY WINKLEBACKER</u> | *Published: OCTOBER 31, 2018* | <u>*Edit*</u>

My much-publicised public humiliation in the Town hall went exactly as I expected. I could have sold the little old wooden horse on my table a thousand times. Sometimes I think the herd are afraid of books, but there again, a few points were scored. Thank goodness Agent Gladstone came to my rescue. "You're only just beginning to make a name for yourself," she chirped. "Oh, by the way, I'm having a break, so I won't be able to keep an eye on all your writing until I receive further instructions."

I'm afraid Gladstone's glory days administering ECST to the scum of the earth are far behind her now.

She has to content herself with lion-taming, or working out-on-the-field. Occasionally we have a chat over lunch. Think of it as a kind of 'social experiment,' I say. Never trust anyone who has mad-eyes, and who goes quiet every time they see you. A lot of people have mental health problems over time. 'Remember your oath of allegiance. The lodge requires that you be silent on all matters relating to your indoctrination. We are fighting to save the world from anyone who's a stiff.'

Gladstone became very pale and nodded. Sometimes I wonder if she's really listening. There are times when I think she could even be pulling my leg.

Hi Andy

I've not 'reported' your books to anyone and have no intention of doing so; it's not my business. I don't know about some of the other *friends* though. We thought that on Thursday you might like to hear what attending the Quaker Meeting means to a few of us and consider what it might mean for you. I never talk about anyone behind their back or through e-mails. In Friendship

Blob

The intolerable life of a Queen

By <u>BIRD DUNG</u> | *Published: NOVEMBER 2, 2018* | <u>*Edit*</u>

We heard from a close confidante of the Queen today about why she was so in love with her corgis.

"Her corgis are the only thing which makes her awful life bearable," she stated, in a very well-spoken and clear voice.

"Even her sons and daughters have to curtsy when they meet her!"

Comments

Dear Sir Norman,

What were MP's doing in the aftermath of the Julian Cole assault by British police officers? In this instance I don't think they can blame it on any 'act of terrorism.' Is this yet another case of people turning a blind eye, and not wanting to get involved. Why were these power-hungry clowns able to get away with their lies for so long. Why are the powers that be so reluctant to criticise these 'friends of the Establishment?' (I am not expecting any kind of reply by the way. Which is exactly the reason why this sort of incident goes unpunished in a so-called liberal society). NO ANSWER.

Caught in the act

By SURLOIN STEAK | Published: OCTOBER 29, 2018 | Edit

I was accosted in the Town hall today by an elderly lady who mentioned my newspaper article and said she had already read two of my books. She would not tell me which ones or make any other comment about them except "interesting...from a psychological point of view. An unusual title. It's not very nice to be 'stalked.'"

Of course, I was never given the chance to ask who was stalked. Had the stalker been stalked by their stalker??
"Do you have a background in psychology?" I asked. "Were you a piss-perfect school teacher..."

"Do you speak from *personal experience,* or are you just another one of the sheep?"
Lurking nearby a rather strange gentleman strode to the table.

"I know you!" he said. "You always wear dark glasses."

"That's because I'm totally insane," I said, "now fk off! Anyway, isn't it time for your Probation appointment?"

*Had I been given the chance before the woman scurried away I would have told her that I thoroughly disapproved of unwanted attention from someone . I have never understood why anyone would want to go after someone who doesn't want them. Where I do part company with the Establishment is how to deal with this when it happens. In a lot of cases of so-called 'stalking,' I don't think any serious harm is intended. Many cases of so-called stalking are not at all malicious.

PAIN-IN-THE-BUTT

I know what you said but who else can I talk to…
mum has developed a habit of 'swigging' from the milk carton.
I asked her not to do it so she threw the leather purse I
bought her into my room...?
awaiting meal at Garden centre I went outside
saw mum go round to my bag and begin going through its contents
she found my collection of keys on my key-ring and took them out
at that point I knocked on the window…
mum held each end up to her chin to make them look like a beard!

She's taken all the friggin keys again!

'That girl you called a slut in class today had just given the head-teacher a bloody good blow-job. The pregnant girl you shouted at across the road has been on the game for years. The boy you called a 'cripple' had just stolen your bicycle. He has to break into houses every night to fund his drug habit. That girl you pushed in the supermarket queue had just stolen from your hand-bag. The girl you called fat has just finished eating her fourth hamburger. The old man you made fun of because of his ugly scars is a former mugger and serial rapist. The boy you saw crying in the street just had the crap beaten out of him for being a bully. You think you know them. Well, yes you do.'

FROM ADVICE AND QUERIES handbook

'Advice and queries are not a call to increased activity by each individual Friend but a reminder of the insights of the Society. Within the community there is a diversity of gifts. We are all therefore asked to consider how far the advices and queries affect us personally and where our own service lies.'

Hi Sue

Nice to see you at the meeting today. All is well or as it should be.

I just wanted to mention one or two things. You probably know anyway.

1 I gave Clive an article to read. If I had read something like that about him I would have responded with care and sincerity, yet not a word. If you can't react or say something to a thing like that then going to the Meeting house is all a sham. We don't meet there just for chairs and coffee. I might just forget I gave it to him.

2 I don't know how she found out, or who told her, I can only guess. Anne has been stalking/monitoring me on my site and has also tracked me down to my Facebook account. I'm not sure if someone has helped her do it because it isn't even under my ordinary name. The odd thing is, her insulting posts have suddenly been removed, although not by me. It will probably be the control freaks at Big Brother again, but who knows. I feel Vicky has issues with me due to her very rigid views. Do you think she has been running to anyone?

Bob probably knows all about it. You know how these things work.

PEACE AND BLESSING

LETTER TO BRAIN

Dear Brian,

Sorry I can't be with you today. I'd just like to explain why. I do care about you. I've never done anything wrong to you. The last time I was over there after we had been out to Yarmouth, you wouldn't play Monopoly with us and kept disappearing round to your neighbours. When you came back your eyes were all red. I was worried you had been listening to stories emanating from Jackie Menagerie down at Bure Valley Crap-house. I hope you haven't been listening to them because they talk a load of old rubbish.

When your mum looked after Sophia while you went to hospital she did you both a favour. She had waited all day for you to come home and was never going to leave Sophia on her own. Yvonne was very rude to her when she came to the door. Your mum said she wouldn't talk to her again until she apologised. According to your mum Yvonne said to her: "You haven't let *him* in the house have you?"

What are you worried I might do Brian?

I hope you had a Happy Easter. Sorry your piles have come back. Must be all that sitting around at your play station and thinking up ways to annoy your mum.

At the moment I don't feel ready to come across. Its not the smell from the decaying stools at the back of the sofa which is really putting me off. I didn't like the atmosphere much the last time I was there and I don't want to put myself in any danger, but I am happy for your mum to keep coming and seeing her grand daughter, even if it is: to be insulted, to have her hair pulled, to be knee'd in the groin and to be spat on.

P~S I hear you have bought a remote control for your toy helicopter. May I wish you many happy hours of enjoyment while the rest of us are out working or earning our bread.

 Ever heard of a scourer?

Paul Gambocini

By RUMPLESTILTSKIN | *Published: NOVEMBER 3, 2018* | *Edit*

Why is it that rich people get huge cash pay-outs while poor people get sent to prison? For years the pigs gloated over his demise. The only time a Member of Parliament takes any interest is when its their name on the charge sheet.

God knows

By RUMPLESTILTSKIN | *Published: NOVEMBER 3, 2018* | *Edit*

I saw Debbie on the path and told her everything.

"Don't worry! God knows," she said. "God knows everything."

Oh, so there is one then?

New Gate-keeper required

By SURLOIN STEAK | *Published: NOVEMBER 4, 2018* | *Edit*

Must be conversant in all forms of communication, carpentry and observation.

When bombing is right

By <u>GODFREY WINKLEBACKER</u> | *Published: NOVEMBER 6, 2018* | *Edit*

I have been told on numerous occasions that I am promoting violence. Let me just say;
I am not the Government, and I don't go around bombing anyone!
Neither do I encourage hurting people. I leave the police to beat people up, fake their reports, and let the Establishment suck up to their deeds.
These monstrous cretins once tried to give me a label based on a painting I had once done of a naked female. They complained I had painted a woman's breast, and that I was therefore some kind of monster. Look in the mirror if you want to see a monster you ugly warped b.asards!
In 1915 Emmeline Pankhurst and three friends stole into a Politician's house to plant some bombs. It nearly blew the place apart. God knows where they got the explosive from.
The Government did a deal with her because they wanted women to contribute to the war effort (making bombs and killing Germans) so they agreed to free her and give women the vote.
In these tolerant and peaceful times many men of Asian origin have been given life sentences based on a few drawings, a piece of string and an old firework.
.ANKER JUDGES!

'THE MAN WHO LOVED WOMEN, by Francoise Truffaut, a very funny film. I saw it years ago. These days the man would be arrested for his behaviour. It's really all about Truffaut himself.'

Dear Alastair Secular

Any chance of a top speaker coming to Aylsham one day soon...?
So sick of the churches dominating everyone round here.
They hire their own speakers to brain-wash people all over town.
The Town hall would be the ideal place.

LOOK WHAT I'VE JUST FOUND

THUNDERBUCK
RAM 1°
éyán doyRá

ISBN
0 9 529896
70

A JOURNEY INTO DARKNESS?

Gambo

The only appliance which gives you what you want exactly when you want it

- Completely self-contained
- No maintenance required
- Free to float in your swimming-pool
- Does not crack all your crazy paving
- Can be de-activated at a moment's notice
- Unable to launch attack missiles
- Able to be kept under lock and key
- Safe to use in your bedroom
- Animal friendly and co-operative

What on earth is going on in this world/country? I post a criticism of the authorities and Government and their sickening hypocrisy on Face-book, and my page gets taken down. No explanation. No apology. No feedback. Isn't there anyone who can do anything about these counts? Best not ask any Politicians. They won't do anything. They won't have a clue what I'm talking about.... *November 7 2018*

Bibles into war

By SURLOIN STEAK | Published: NOVEMBER 5, 2018 | Edit

A young soldier who was saved from shrapnel by his bible said:
"I was never happier than when I carried my bible off to war. I always kept it in my right-hand pocket until the good Lord told me to move it to my left pocket. I was protected from the full impact of the shell by my pocket bible while the other heathens were ripped apart."
When asked why some of his Christian friends died alongside him too he said that they had refused to listen to the Good lord and had not moved their bible over to the right pocket...?

Agent Crowther

By PETER SMITH | Published: NOVEMBER 4, 2018 | Edit

I spoke to Agent Crowther down at the dog track today. He's racing his pedigree greyhound 'Daisy' in the three o'clock classic. Crowther is quite a small person in comparison to myself. While Gladstone is tall, Crowther is extremly short, almost a midget. Crowther wanted to know who my main influences were: Harry H Corbett, Frank Ifield, Bridget Bardot, the Milk marketing board etc...

After that he walked away and began chatting to Gladstone again.

A few seconds later Gladstone marched over to where I was standing. She was extremely impatient and rude. I could hardly get a word in edge-ways.

"I never said you had mad eyes. That was someone else!"

She screamed through her mega-phone.

After she had calmed down a bit she walked towards the door and knocked her head on the door lintel.

As soon as she left Crowther came to stand with me again;

"I'm very fussy who I invite round for coffee," he said. "I don't really like Gladstone very much. She is too close to the Gate-keeper for my liking. The old Gate-keeper has suddenly become very chatty. We will have to get rid of her."

He eye-pointed towards Geoffrey who was making everyone a drink, mocking his public-school accent.

"Those that can, do, and those that can't teach!" he laughed.

"I've heard that Geoffrey is flying out to Texas to see if he can help kick those flea-infested carts back into the Rio Grande?"

"I wouldn't be too worried about the caravans," sighed Crowther, "I would be more worried about Becky getting me on my own…!"

Hi Jonathan…

NO problem. was a bit disappointed, but hey, that's life.
No David, no Matt. Must have gone to the bonfire.
That little guy you were playing seemed scared to look at me.

Whatever have I done to him… ☹
This is all since I told you about my books…
Isn't there a tournament in Lowestoft, with an International
Grand Master entering? I might be interested, but there are only
forty places. Its not that far away.
Yep, a lot of faces missing tonight. I ran
a small Writing group a while back and you just never knew who
was going to turn up…apart from the pigs.

To Sarah Price, retired mental health nurse…'you will never be old, so long as you let me teach you how to feed the donkeys.'

Holier than thou hypocrites

BONFIRE NIGHT

Cold on the place of thunder

Summer burning hot,
in the sauna of the carriage,
as we journey south, together,
The clatter of wheels,
Under our feet.

She turns, and rests, her body,
blonde on the leather...
Hoists up her legs,
Her voice calm before sunset.

With knees pushed to her rib-cage,
The blue denim tight on her hips,
Her hands clutched to the handbag,
In the pale night of oblivion.

Cold, cold on the place of thunder,
Her lips solemn and full,
Her eyes closed to the world,
When suddenly I spring to life.

Cold, cold on the place of thunder,
Our skin touches,
With the faint *stick* of moisture,
Jammed up to the hold.

Before the night scream gored,
And I was thrown to the earth,
in a gust of disgust.

Had I remained, still as a hawk,
The heavens may not have opened,
Cold, cold where my love lay,
In the travelling car,
On the way to the dungeon of dreams.

Contempt for the iron horse

I fought my way across the field,
Angry with what I'd made,
And heard you steaming in the forest,
Your nostrils flared and your breath,
burning like fire.

When your bulk raced,
Round the headland to greet me,
I prepared myself for war,
The thud,
Of your steel drum,
your metal shaft,
And wheels of thunder.

Blasting on your horn to restrain me,
I felt your weight above me,
And slung you into the heavens,
Peering upwards,
At the watching stars.

Holding the dearest things to my heart,
I looking away for one instant,
To see you had already been and gone,
Leaving a river of scarlet.

LIES LIES AND MORE LIES

Occupant:

Re. Notification of application for an Injunction

We are receiving continued reports that your behaviour is interfering with the peaceful enjoyment by other residents of their homes. Residents at Bure Valley House are vulnerable due to age and disability. The level of distress being caused mean it is appropriate for me to collate evidence to put in place an injunction to prevent you from continuing in these acts of Anti-Social Behaviour. As a responsible landlord we have a duty of care towards our tenants and are taking this action in the interests of those adversely affected by your behaviour.

The incidents reported by residents of Bure Valley House of Anti-Social Behaviour by you include reports of noise nuisance emanating from 39 Bure Valley House while you are visiting the property. Also you continue to cycle on the footpaths around Bure Valley House despite verbal requests and then written instructions from Circle Housing Wherry not to do so.

Wherry has also received complaints that you are not dressed adequately while in public areas on the scheme including while carrying out physical exercises in front of residents windows in the communal gardens. Due to the level of distress this behaviour is causing to other residents I believe it would be reasonable to request that you wear clothing which covers your upper torso when in the communal parts of the scheme including the grounds. This is to avoid alarm and distress to other residents who are not comfortable with your state of undress.

An example of the distress caused by your behaviour is illustrated by an incident which occurred in the communal reading room at Bure Valley House on 1st January 2015 at 1.30pm. A resident walked into this public room while you were in a state of undress. You were with an unidentified person and were perceived to be performing a sexual act in a public place. The resident concerned has been deeply upset by this incident.

'

Don't trust anyone!

By HERPES ZOSTER | Published: NOVEMBER 7, 2018 | Edit

Especially when it's one of the do-gooding control-freaks down at the Busybodies bizarre. Nice to your face alright but:

- talking behind your back
- undermining you wherever they can
- preaching love and forgiveness
- sneaking to the Authorities
- brown nosing round each other
- some more than others!

Prince Charles the Chicken-heart

By USULI TWELVES | Published: NOVEMBER 9, 2018 | Edit

What won't a royal do to hold onto the castle and all its privileges. Prince Charles has agreed to button his lip, in return for a crown and the chance to sit on the throne.

He's agreed 'never to express his opinion on any subject he feels strongly about.' Have you ever heard anything so ridiculous? This is tantamount to the Anglican church keeping quiet about the Trump presidency. Aren't we all subjects of the king...

I guess he thinks the media will give him an easier life, but I wouldn't bank on it.

I met a lady travelling south on the train towards London many years ago. She was about my age. I think she was in between jobs or teaching. I told her I was trying to get some work published and that I was interested in being a Writer. She said that she too aspired to be an Author and that she had already written copious amounts of work but didn't know what to do next. We talked a lot about books and literature. I encouraged her to try and get her work published, as I intended to do.

HER NAME: J K ROWLING.

JUST THE BEGINNING

Holly rubbed her eyes and stared at her alarm.

"Time to get up already...Oh, no-o-o!"

She screwed up her face and pulled the duvet over her head.

Holly could hear her mother calling from the bottom of the stairs...

"Are you up yet, lazy bones?"

'Why do I have to go to school. Why is school so frigging boring? I don't even want to be there!'

A few seconds later her door was flung open and her mother rushed to the bed. She dragged the duvet from her daughter and grabbed her by the throat.

"This is the last time you get *me* into Court! You *little minx.*"

Her mother threw her clothes from the chair.

"If you aren't dressed in five minutes I'm throwing you out of the house. I have to sign on at the dole office. When I get back you won't be here!"

Her mother's head was clean shaven. She had a stud on her tongue and an ear-ring through her nose. For the last seventeen months she'd been having hormone therapy to see if she could finally get rid of her breasts.

"I'm tired. I haven't even had time to put on my make-up."

Holly yawned and swung her shapely legs over the side of the bed.

"Bully!"

Her mother slapped her full in the face, then skipped out of the room to put on her bomber jacket.

Holly began to cry. Then she remembered what day it was.

'St. Margaret's Roman Catholic convent school had been run by nuns for the last fifty years. Classes were full of unruly teenage girls. Every day the teachers were confronted by a mob of hissing and abusive young women. Anyone who wanted to learn had to put up with hours of chaos while the teacher who was supposed to be in charge nearly had a nervous break-down. The Headmistress spent most of the day locked up in her own study with a bottle of brandy. Drugs were freely available at the school gate as young hoodlums walked their girlfriends to the entrance pushing their prams.'

"Mum, why isn't there ever anything in this landfill for breakfast?"

"Get it yourself. You know where the shop is."

She heard the slam of the door as her mother scrambled out.

All was quiet, until she noticed a dark silhouette through the glass.

When she opened the door, Tony was standing on the door-step grinning.

He pushed his way inside and grabbed her hand on the way up to the bedroom.

As she lay on her back Holly could hear him grunting and groaning on top of her.

She wondered if dad was okay. It would soon be visiting day. She still loved him, no matter what he'd done...to improve her education.

(Re-written for Sherie June 2018)

Portraiture

Whenever the light is on,
My ugly face appears,
Down in the water.

Its crude and intemperate lines,
Stare up at me from the fog,
Of my own urine.

Each lovely image,
With its wooden frame,
Greets me whenever,
I come to stay,
In this house.

Dearest Rolf,

I'm writing to tell you how wonderful it is to be rolling in cash while you are rotting in a filthy stinking prison cell. We have been out on the sands again today and have bought another surf board to stand alongside the others.

Susan hasn't written to me for many months. I miss her full and frank communication. My son has just arrived back from his fishing expedition. Bill has been out to cut the lawn. We now have three wonderful grand-children.

Let me be frank.: I greatly appreciate the time we spent surreptitiously bonking in the dark. It was extremely enjoyable and gave me a fantastic lesson in human biology. Your syrupy shaggy-haired cock is the best functioning weapon I have ever had the pleasure of screwing. I hope it is still functioning well and giving you lots of happy hours. We often talk about you and the moments we spent together on the sofa while the old bitch was kipping upstairs. My partner has instructed me to come as many times as I can manage thinking about it. Sorry about dragging your name through the mud, but it made us all laugh hysterically.

Sincerely,

A Sunny-Beach

"There are no tell-tales in our town"

When I came back from the chess club tonight Kingsmill was waiting for me in the driveway. He was wearing a long Great-coat and a face mask which he'd stolen from a kid at the local bus-shelter. He was panting as if he'd just done a mile sprint round the block with Usain Bolt.

"I have something really urgent to tell you," he said, "and you aren't going to like it one little bit. It is not ethically correct and goes completely against any decent honourable standards of behaviour. It could even involve greed and the pursuit of power. Something we absolutely deplore and have been attempting to expunge from the planet in more than three hundred years of procrastination."

"If it's about Gladis having one of her grandsons named after Adolf Hitler, I've already heard. I haven't seen much of her since she ran off with the odd Gate-keeper. That was just before the new chairs arrived. I think they were far too small for her arse."

"She was becoming very disruptive again too," he whimpered. "Even Becky said so. We were close to having her confined to the garden or a part of the building which was quiet and less likely to trigger one her bitter outbursts. She stole one of books from the library and won't give it back to us. A thumb screw might be the only alternative in order to reinforce our strict moral dictum."

"Gladstone's a Sex-offender!" Crowther suddenly blurted. "A morally reprehensible human being, with only a minute speck of the God-factor within her."
The bowler hat he was wearing spun round, and flew off his head into a nearby turnip field. A mixture of spit and saliva covered my face.

"Try not to jump to conclusions," I said, "we may be slightly off the mark, and anyway, Becky has some very serious problems of her own, which I won't go into unless you really want me to."

"Oh, my goodness. What did she actually do?" I queried.

"One of the Alders found her knelt on the lavatory floor sniffing a toilet seat!" he gleamed.

"Well, I never knew she was like that," I said. "This is hardly the behaviour of someone with honesty and integrity. The time has come to start giving her the treatment she deserves. We will smile sweetly at her, talk to her as if we don't know what she has been up to but keep our distance, and plan what to do with her the next time Geoffrey is out shooting bunny rabbits. I recommend aversion therapy, or at the very least, a nice frenzied exorcism."

Biography

Born into an ill-informed inebriate family with both parents at constant loggerheads in 1956. Brainwashed at a Catholic indoctrination centre from the age of four. Regularly ordered to leave home by his father because he didn't belong there. Consistent beatings and mental abuse for several years. Visited his father in a psychiatric hospital at the age of eleven. Mother even more barmy and controlling. Punished for not going to the toilet at the age of eighteen. Became socio-phobic while still in the sixth form. Fell in love but was rejected due to poor height ratio. Attended Art college but was considered too mad by his contempories. Came into conflict with society from an early age and was fined for flashing his penis at a group of Carol Singers who had called at his home. Went bald at the age of twenty-one and remained a virgin well into middle-age. Made his name as a physical culturist and naturist. In 2007 was sent to prison after being caught in possession of a fire-arm. The rifle and hand-grenades were never unearthed...

- o Teacher of Sign-language
- o British Rail Signalman and Guard
- o Art therapist
- o Good Samaritan
- o Short story Writer and satirist
- o Social commentator of world renown
- o Award winning poet and Author

"I am not biased in any way. My judgements are based solely on what is right and what is just not popular with the public" Judge Jeremy Bum-bandit Scoff: Ass-hole and High Court, The Capital Land of (plenty). "The Government is always right, even when they're wrong" Sir Stephen P. Lock: Scapegoat Supplies Ltd., Food bank Road, Birmingham. "The most shocking and disgusting thing I have ever read" Lord Peter Ebensraum von Ribbentrop Ribbentrop: Chief Organist, Munich, Once-was-Germany. "It riles me to say it, but there is genius in this work!" Lady Celia Frank-winkle Fosse: Shoreditch and District Snots, The Sikh Temple, Poorly People's Lane, Monmouth. "We've seen and heard enough of this to last a lifetime" Rabbi Mannie Cold-well: Seventh Synagogue, Best-Placein-town, HOLLYWOOD BOULEVARD. "Not of the common herd!" Carlos Nagual Castaneda: Wizard, Rose from the dead and was buried, Jumping Clouds, Mexico. "Where is a stick of dynamite when you need one?" Jack D: Under Review. Can't decide which path: NO CONTEST. "Helped to construct our first home made device" Abdul Karim: Poet, New York Subway, INCOGNITO. "Sent us his work and we sent it back!" Jerk the Johnson Publishers Inc.: Did not fit in with our current cata - logue: Standards-have-to-be maintained, Plymouth, UK. "A book which completely epitomises the current zeitgeist" Stacey Waddington-Goose: Exorcist, Airport Lounge Road, Hong Kong. Top customer reviews 5.0 out of 5 stars. 'An unusual, highly original voice. Quite an extraordinary collection of poems, recollections, short scenes and illustrations. This is a deeply satisfying, provocative, anti-authoritarian celebration of life. Fragments of letters and dialogue from scattered, overheard conversations, present a vision of the world that is highly original - humorous and subversive. I have not been challenged by any writing so much in years.' Dr Leon Zeilig, Professor: Johannesburg, S.A.